Inspiralled

a collection of prose and poetry

by

Pen and Paper

The Bromley House Writing Group

First published by the Pen and Paper Writing Group in the United Kingdom in 2024

ISBN no. 978-1-917010-81-8

Cover design and text by Pen and Paper

Illustrations by: Jessica Adams (p. 35); Mike Carter (pp. 3, 7, 38, 43, 46, and 50), and Guy Kiddey (pp. 53 and 56)

Pen and Paper Group photos page by Greg Williams

Edited by Mike Carter, assisted by the other members of Pen and Paper

A copy of this book is held by the British Library

Printed by the Ashford Press

CONTENTS

Janet Gibson

Barry Harper

Julia Hodson

Lindah Kiddey

Chris Niven

Marcus Nolan

Mike O'Sullivan

Sarah Payler

Mark Pringle

Cindy Rossiter

The Contributors

Foreword by Clare Brown

On alternate Tuesday mornings, a group of Bromley House Library members meet to spend a morning discussing, developing and sharing their writing. Part technical workshop, part creative arena, these sessions have challenged and inspired the writers to push the boundaries of their craft. This collection gives us a glimpse into that engine room, which has produced fiction, poetry, prose and memoir, and a taste of the invention, wit and skill which characterises their work. There are also some charming illustrations by Mike Carter, Guy Kiddey and Jessica Adams.

Writers have been free to choose their own forms and themes, and this collection reflects their wide and varied interests. Travel writing and personal anecdote sit beside suspenseful stories and poignant poems; multiple casts of characters - including several animals, real and mythical – play out their dramas on the page. And while there is no shying away from sadness and loss, an undercurrent of humour – life-affirming, rebellious, sometimes sardonic – is rarely far away.

I suspect this is, at least in part, because members of Pen and Paper spend every other alternate Tuesday morning, the ones between their Bromley House sessions, enjoying one another's company in Nottingham's coffee shops and occasionally on cultural walks and visits. The friendships and social bonds within the group underpin their creative endeavours and make this collection a genuine labour of love. Thank you from Bromley House Library to all the writers who contributed to its publication.

This is a book to dip into and find something new to enjoy every time.

Clare Brown

Library Director

Simon Allen

Grandad You're a Boomer

An unfinished and unpolished villanelle from a quick exercise at a Bromley House Library writing group session.

Grandad you just don't understand
It's not like it was in your day
You really lived in another land

Yours was a world you could command
The same dark forces were not at play
Grandad you just don't understand

Life then could be better planned
Over your fate you had some sway
You really lived in another land

Your future laid out in cards fanned
You didn't have to beg or pray
Grandad you just don't understand

I feel I'm on shifting sand
I cannot tell the night from day
You really lived in another land

But I do welcome your helping hand
Even when you hear me say
Grandad you just don't understand
You really lived in another land

Mike Carter

The Sunlit Cafe

This piece was inspired by Edward Hopper's painting 'A Sunlit Cafe'.

A woman sits alone in a cafe, bathed in the mid-morning sunlight that is streaming through the window. The street outside is in shadow. A pigeon waddles along the pavement. Then another flutters noisily down and makes his way towards her. She takes off and settles on a windowsill. He flies up to join her. She takes off yet again, flying further out of reach.

The woman has just been served with a coffee. 'That's it, I've just about had it with men. Right now I just want to be left on my own.'

The man in the dark blue jacket looks across at her. 'It's must be my lucky day. She's here on her own and looking for a man.'

She notices him out of the corner of her eye. 'Oh no, he's looking my way. Any minute now he's going to try and make conversation.'

'It's up to me to make the first move. I must remember to play it cool.'

'Any minute now he's going to come up with some dumb-assed opener.'

'Wow - I can't take my eyes off that blue dress she's wearing.'

'Would you believe it? He's staring at my breasts. Can't a woman wear a nice summer dress without some pervert ogling her?'

'I love the way her long red hair is catching the sunlight. Reminds me of Rita Hayworth.'

'Yuk, his hair's really greasy, and his collar's covered in dandruff.'

He reaches into his jacket pocket, 'I'll offer her a *Lucky Strike*. That will impress her.'

'Oh, he's not going to light up, is he? I can't stand the smell of cigarettes. They ought to ban smoking in public places!'

The revolving door in the corner starts to move. A second woman makes her entrance. The red-haired woman turns around to greet her.

'There you are, Sally. I got your message, so I asked if I could take my lunch break early. Let's go and eat and you can tell me all about it.'

The two women make their way out into the street. Back inside the cafe, the man lights a cigarette.

'That was bad luck. I would have been in there if her friend hadn't arrived. I'll just have to order another coffee and see if any more dames show up.'

Outside, Sally tucks her arm under the sleeve of her friend's jacket. 'Thank God you came when you did. Did you see that creep sitting opposite me? I'm sure he was just about to make a move.'

'What, the one who looked like Norman Bates out of *Psycho*?'

'Yes, that's the one. Well, I won't be checking into his motel in a hurry!'

The two women burst out laughing and walk away arm in arm. Meanwhile, the pigeon resumes his position on a first floor windowsill on the other side of the street.

Doorstepped

A man strolled up my drive
dressed in his Sunday best,
the Bible in his hand,
conviction in his breast.

'I bring Good News,' he said,
'It's written in this book.
'The Lord has come to save us all.
Why don't you take a look?'

I said,'I have some questions
if you can spare the time -
there's something's not quite right
and it's preying on my mind.'

'Is God the Creator of everything,
all-knowing and all-powerful besides,
caring for the poor and sick?'
'Why, of course,' the man replied.

'Well, if God has created everything,
then it is he who is to blame
for the foulest of diseases
that inflicted so much pain.'

'If God is so omnipotent,
why did he not see her tears,
reach out his hand to comfort her,
not take away her years?'

'And why would a benevolent god
cause a blameless one to suffer?
with all the evil in the World,
Why could he not choose another?'
'

And how could a caring father
have his son nailed to a cross
to atone for Mankind's every sin?
I'm completely at a loss!'

So don't you dare to tell me
God moves in a mysterious way.'
Having said my piece, I closed the door.
There was nothing more to say.

Byron at 8 St James's Street

In 1808 the poet Byron went to
London, where he stayed in hotels
and lodgings for the next four years.
Between 1808-9 and 1811-12 he
stayed at 8 St James Street in rooms
above a hatter's shop. The hatter
was my fourth great grandfather
Francis Dollman, who became
involved in a notable incident.

St. James's was, and is still, a
very fashionable street, situated
between Piccadilly and Pall Mall.
Dollman's clientele included
members of the Royal Family and
the Aristocracy. Next door was Lock
& Co., another up-market hatters,
who are still in business today.

Byron was in the process of selling his home at Newstead
Abbey, preferring a rootless, but more exciting life in London. In

1812 he became an instant celebrity when his new poem *Childe Harold* sold out in three days. As he later recalled, "I awoke one morning and found myself famous.' I can imagine Byron, upstairs at 8 St James Street, reading through a pile of congratulatory letters, while Francis Dollman was busy selling hats on the ground floor.

One of Byron's new admirers was Lady Caroline Lamb, the wife of the future prime minister Lord Melbourne. In the summer of 1812 they began an affair. She did all the running, often waiting out in the street for him to come home from late night parties. The pair decided to elope, but then Byron got cold feet.

One day, he and his friend John Cam Hobhouse were about to set off on a trip to Harrow when a 'thunderous knocking' was heard downstairs. A crowd gathered in the street to see what was happening. It was Lady Caroline, concealed under a cloak. She made her way upstairs to Byron's rooms, while Hobhouse slipped downstairs to buy himself a hat. An enthusiastic cross-dresser, Lady Caroline was wearing the livery of one of her pages. She was small, thin and rather boyish looking, which was how Byron liked his women! A noisy scene ensued. Hobhouse returned upstairs with Dollman, who requested that she be asked to leave, presumably because it was bad for business. Things got very heated. At one point Byron had to hold back his lover as she attempted to grab his dress sword from the sofa. Eventually, she calmed down and agreed to leave.

By the Autumn of 1812 Newstead had been sold and Byron escaped to Cheltenham. It was the end of his time living above my ancestor at 8 St. James's Street, which was later renamed Byron House.

Barry Cope

Last Night of Cowes Regatta

It was not until decades later that I first learned about Utilitarianism. I doubt if Michael Sandell was even born then. This all happened, after all, in an age when it was just assumed that hedonism and utilitarianism emulsified together naturally, like anis and water. Although drinks like Pernod were not part of our usual diet. We drank beer.

That night we were literally afloat surrounded by Guinness barrels, not barrels of Guinness. The sailing fraternity had discovered that empty stout barrels made perfect mooring buoys, but the brewery had yet to act to prevent theft by imposing a swingeing deposit charge on them. Hundreds of the gleaming stainless-steel casks floated in Cowes harbour, each linked to a sunken anchor. Each had a boat tethered to it. Mostly these were sleek racing yachts; a few were comfortable auxiliary cruisers, ours was an exception. It was a clearly functional, ungentrified workboat, carvel built, powered by an inboard petrol engine, and steered by tiller. It was the sort of open boat that could at that time still be found on every beach from Filey to Padstow, painted gaily, but crudely, and named something like Saucy Suzie and offering trips round the bay.

About a dozen of us lay around on the boat's seats taking sips from cans of Gale's Horndean XB bitter. Under one thwart seat a large cardboard carton bulged with screwed-up fish and chip wrappers and empty cans. The final salvo of rockets for the traditional last night of regatta firework display cracked open the sky in a multicoloured floral burst of energy. Last orders had been called in the pubs and we were sated with chips. There was no need to stay further. Most of us needed to be at work in the morning and we faced a trip of a couple of hours before we were home, starting with an hour on the water. Bosun, as we all called the only person on the boat above the age of twenty-five, close-coupled the two-man rowing dinghy that served as a tender. Mike, the technician who ran the test-tank, untied us from our barrel-buoy as soon as Bosun had swung the somewhat temperamental engine into life and resumed his place at the tiller. We puttered slowly along the West Cowes shore, our little work-boat passing along the flanks of whippet-slim inshore racers and under the counters of lordly ocean racers. We must have seriously spoiled the view from the brilliantly-lit Royal Yacht Squadron Clubhouse before we turned north into the Solent.

It had all seemed a good idea at the time. In fact it was still great fun but the air was getting cold and we would have to tidy up the boat and not leave any traces. The Director kept the college shipshape and Bristol fashion; no chip wrappers or beer cans could be left to be discovered by academic staff in the morning. We had slipped Bosun a few pounds and the college launch had been made available. Now it had to be returned. Navigation did not look difficult for a local man like Bosun. In the distance, the vast Esso petrochemical complex, at Fawley on the mainland, lit up the country around as brightly as day. All we had to do was steer a straight course just to the east of the refinery into Southampton Water and then look out for the entrance to the Hamble River- no problem on a calm, clear night.

The boat's engine was built more for torque than speed, rather like the contemporary Phelon and Moore Panther motorbikes that were quite common at the time, and whose engines were said to fire at alternate lamp-posts. The silence of the moonless night was thus only broken by a regular, but infrequent, thump as one of the few cylinders reached the ignition stroke. That is until the engine faltered ….. picked up ….. faltered again ….. picked up, and then expired without further warning. Utter silence followed until much joking about rowing and reliving school and college exploits in shell eights started. Bosun was not laughing as he called for volunteers to assist him. He levered up the engine cover and took out a selection of spanners and a plug-wrench. Someone then noticed a white shape, brilliantly illuminated, far away at the very point that we were aiming for. There was a certain amount of under-the-breath cursing from the engine well whenever a spanner slipped or a torch was misdirected. The white shape grew steadily larger then, as it passed the flares of the refinery it suddenly changed shape from squarish to long and like a cliff.

It was a ship, a very, very big ship, unmistakably a passenger liner. In fact it was a thirty thousand ton P & O liner outward bound from Southampton to Sidney and we were looking at its port side. How graceful she looked, but powerful too, surging ahead fast, a magnificent sight like some mystic barque come to collect a mythical knight. She would seem be no problem to us though; she was clearly heading west to enter into the English Channel between the Needles and Calshot Spit. Our eyes went back to the work being expended on the engine repair, until we noticed that we were once again head-on to the liner. As we watched the ship, now much closer, turned to present her starboard side, she was now clearly heading east to leave the Solent by the Spithead channel. But within seconds she was swinging again.

Suddenly, everything became clear; we were near the Brambles sandbank drifting with any current that might take us. We needed very little water below us; the P & O needed around thirty feet. The pilot was taking the ship through the maze of navigable channels, jinking like a wing-three-quarter. We might easily drift over those channels. The chances of the pilot or any officer on the bridge a hundred feet above sea level and two hundred feet from the bow of the ship seeing us were slight. Had we been spotted the inclination of a captain, even if made aware of our existence, to run thirty thousand tons of expensive and luxuriously fitted steel carrying over a thousand people aground at some speed did not seem likely. Utilitarianism would have come into play and Sandell could have had a real-life example to add to his brake-less bus illustration. We realised that there was a distinct likelihood our boat could be run down and that we could be chopped into mincemeat by the propellers; the few sacrificed for the greater safety of the many. We could imagine the front pages of the next morning's late editions. We would all have been described as brilliant students and young people at the start of promising careers. Our families would have told how we could light up rooms by our very presence and how kind we were to animals and those less fortunate than ourselves.

As it happened no-one needed to perjure themself. Bosun tightened up a spare set of spark-plugs and, just when RMS Arcadia was looking far too close for comfort, we were under way, out of her way, faster than the launch had moved for decades.

Two Sides of Greece

There is nowhere around the Mediterranean that compares with the harsh beauty of the Mani peninsula. An ambiguous Greek saying is "bring me a stone from the Mani". There is not much else to bring .The Mani is nothing but pure, unyielding stone, fringed by olive groves.

It is a region of extremes; devastatingly hot in summer, cruelly cold and stormy in winter. In early spring the olive groves are ablaze with the colour of a carpet of wild flowers: yellow, purple, scarlet and white. It is impossible to set a foot down without crushing anemones. Then, as the Mani's numerous snakes move out of their winter cover to bask in the sun they are picked off by the eagles which drift on thermals up the edges of the mountains on their way north from Africa. Occasionally a skein of pelicans will sweep low over the sea. In March the air is as clear as gin in daytime and the sun blazes; at night there is a cold dankness that makes a wood-fire essential indoors, and two fleeces vital when outside. There is no need for a weather forecast. If, in early morning, two fighter aircraft from Kalamata scream down the coast you know that the weather is going to be clear enough for the air force to trust trainees out with serious jets.

Mo and I love the Mani in spring, and have made several trips there, walking in the mountains all day and going down to the village in the evening for salt fish or musakka and ouzo. Usually we take a late afternoon flight back from Athens, a schedule which demands a pre-dawn start from our base village of Lefktron. We stand in the dark, beside the domed church, feeling the air palpably warming from bracing to velvet with every passing minute as sunrise approaches, and looking anxiously down to the coast, waiting to catch the headlights of the taxi from Kardamili as it climbs the dirt road from the coast to collect us. It is vital that we get to Kalamata, the southernmost terminus of the railway, in time for the first train to Athens.

One year we decided to fulfil an old ambition and make a one-night stop-over in Athens to permit a visit to Cape Sounion. I had wanted to see this most romantic of ruins ever since I had been sent a post-card of it by a school friend years ago. Particularly I wanted to see the column in the temple of Poseidon where Lord Byron had so ironically incised his name in the stone after writing about the unblemished beauty of the 'marbled steep'.

Railway timetables everywhere often have an element of fiction about them. On the seven hour journey south we had been promised a buffet service, but none was provided. We arrived tired, hungry and thirsty. We had thus provisioned for the return trip with bread, olives, feta, salami, oranges and retsina.   Needless to say as soon as the train cleared the suburbs of Kalamata the food trolley started circulating.

The route is a romantic historian's delight. The train stops at Nemea, where Hercules slew the lion; Tripolis, where Oedipus was posed the riddle; Argos; Corinnth, and Mycenae. During the dull final run into the capital, I spent my time studying the Rough Guide, looking for affordable accommodation between the Peleponnesos Railway Station and Areos Park, whence we would need to catch the first bus out to Sounion at eight in the morning. I found just the place. It was described as being comfortable, cheap, friendly and tolerant of back-packers. When we arrived in Athens we strode out with visions of having a shower and a rest before hitting the Plaka for an end of mission meal. There was no difficulty in finding the address, and the name above the door was as expected. The place didn't look quite as we had expected though.

We had envisaged several possibilities, faded nineteenth century elegance perhaps, YHA style earnestness, or maybe student flophouse informality. Instead the effect was decidedly 'footballers' wives'. It was clearly under new ownership. The exterior walls had been clad with a sandy-beige marble, flecked with black. An orange carpet covered the steps leading up from the pavement to the reception door. The door, like the windows, was glazed with the sort of dark glass specified by drug-dealers for their BMW 4x4s, and the handles were massive bronze castings. We went into the lobby, where a bulky grey-haired man of indeterminate age sat behind a huge and highly polished rosewood desk whose top was unnaturally empty. His wrists and neck were weighed down by heavy gold jewellery. His purple silk shirt was open almost to the waist to display luxuriant chest hair.

Mo was in the lead and she asked for a double room. No problem. She then strained her self-taught Greek explaining that we only needed it for one night. The manager looked surprised at this and suggested that one hour would be normal, perhaps two, even three, but all night! The drachma then dropped as to what even friendlier establishment this friendly hotel had become.

I have often wondered what the proprietor thought of us. I am sure that he had seen many different tastes catered for there; S & M, rubber-wear, uniforms; but a middle-aged couple in walking clothes and boots, carrying large rucksacks, must surely have struck him as being slightly out of the ordinary. Perhaps he thought that the bags contained exceptionally large quantities of specialised equipment for some arcane northern practices.

We left hurriedly, without even making excuses, and eventually found a conventional hotel a few streets away in Victory Square. Even that, though, had an unusual option for those not entertained by English Premiership football on television. Admittedly other choices included a Greek version of Blind Date, but the real surprise was in the form of a very classy, and totally free, hard-core porn channel. They do things differently abroad, sometimes very differently.

I Met Charlie's Driver

In the mid 2000s, Sue, our daughter-in-law's mother had a holiday home, a thatched cottage that had once been a school, in Dolton, a village right in the middle of Devonshire. Needless to say when we were invited to spend a few days there with Sue and Nigel, her second husband, we didn't think twice. The evening that we arrived Nigel asked if we had noticed the stud farm as we drove along the link to Dolton from the main Exeter to Barnstable road. That, he explained, was where Charlie and Shirley lived and where she bred her beloved horses. They were, he said, not exactly reclusive, they did use the village facilities, but they kept a low profile.

I got on very well with Nigel. He was some years older than me and from a different social background, but we had a lot in common, inevitably. Inevitably because we were both part of a cohort of British males who graduated from infancy between the great depression of the 1930s and the death throes of the Empire consequent upon the Suez fiasco of 1956. Boys who started school in those twenty-five or so years were trained to believe that Britain was still the greatest world power and would eternally be the Workshop of the World. The economy was coal-fired and industry was heavy, tuning out machinery, ships, cars, lorries and railway locomotives for lesser nations. Technology involved big lumps of iron, not invisible electrons.

We read Hotspur and Wizard, comics full of racialism, xenophobia and misogyny, whose influence those of us lucky enough to get a decent education, mainly courtesy of the Butler Act, worked hard to eradicate. We also studied the cutaway drawings that exposed the details of construction of the most impressive products of British engineering in the more upmarket and expensive comic Eagle. We spotted trains, steam of course, and we yearned for Hornby train sets. We saved pocket money for Meccano accessories. We bought fretwork kits to make models of English sailing ships, like the

Mayflower, from Hobbies shops and we also made balsa-wood models of early jet aircraft. We learned to recognise every make and model of car. We were a living Flanders and Swan song.

To put things more succinctly, both Nigel and I liked old machinery. Nigel had not only kept the firm's 'Bookmaker's Rolls-Royce' Jaguar when he retired but he also had a soft-top E-type Jaguar as well as an MG TC that he had painstakingly restored from dereliction. I had dabbled with classics only to the extent of having a Triumph Spitfire.

I had told Nigel about an anxious journey to a funeral at Selsey that we had made a few weeks before. A lorry fire had resulted in complete closure of the A34, the normal route to the south coast, and the diversion had landed us in the midst of traffic jams among the crowds heading for the Goodwood Festival of Speed. This was an event which always had thousands of petrol-heads digging out their brick-coloured trousers and string-backed gloves to wear while watching super-rich enthusiasts speeding around the Duke of Richmond's private Formula 1 circuit, which, like his personal horse-race track, was in the grounds of his stately home, Goodwood House, near Chichester. Nigel had then told me that, if I could think of some small electrical item to buy, he would show me one of the cars attracting the enthusiasts to that event. After some thought I concluded that reception on our then new digital radio would be improved by fitting a better aerial, and so we set off for the village centre.

Dolton is a very small village, and it had, at that time, very few shops, perhaps literally three or four, one of which was a distinct oddity. It was a shop that sold and serviced domestic electrical apparatus of all kinds from 3 amp fuse cartridges to full-scale white goods such as freezers and washing machines. We went in and, as slowly as I possibly could, chose an aerial, giving Nigel time to chat to the proprietor and work the subject round to old cars and to establish that he had not only driven up to Goodwood, but had returned the car to storage, as usual, behind the shop after its outing on the track. I was then drawn back into the conversation and it was arranged that the shop counter would be left in the charge of the proprietor's wife while we three went through the yard to inspect the contents of the store.

Opening the store-room door revealed a dust-sheet made from old curtains. When this was, with due ceremonial flourish, hauled aside, there stood the car. 'Charlie especially likes this one; we always take it to Goodwood, if he's in the country.' It was a splendid sports car. Gloriously glossy, curvy and very dark green, like an extremely ripe smooth-skinned avocado, it was, I believe, a BMW328. This model is described in a standard work on classic cars as 'the best all-rounder you could buy in 1939, and a five-star classic today.' I can't check that identification, as I was strictly forbidden to take any photographs. Whatever it was it was beautiful, smoothly elegant, purposeful and efficient, realistic in style rather than overbearingly pompous like the Mercedes giants favoured by Germany's rulers of the time. 'Charlie's got a bit of a collection, but he doesn't make a fuss about it. He doesn't drive himself, you see, always gets me to do it. He always likes to go to the big classics rallies, unless he's on tour with the Stones, of course.'

Paragon
(as Hamlet might have said)

I was recently able to spend some time observing human behaviour from a relaxed and detached position, a hospital bed. I had the chance to see a constantly changing and moving population of worried men interacting with a small unvarying background group of calm professionals. We, the patients, were concerned with our well-being and our very mortality. This was an acute cardiac facility, we all had disorders of a vital organ that had no back-up. Our hopes of recovery, in some cases of survival, depended on the ability and application of the physicians, nurses, surgeons, technicians, porters and caterers who staffed the Trent Cardiac Unit at Nottingham City Hospital. We were timorous, respectful, grateful to the staff. Or rather all of us were, except one. This one individual enabled us to think of another organ as well as the heart, the anus. He was, undoubtedly, an arsehole, and he was alliteratively called Andrew.

This single exception was a man who for two or three days occupied the bed diametrically opposite mine in a four bed bay. My feelings about him are, I am sure, in no way influenced by the fact that his emergency addition to the operating list meant that I had to spend an extra weekend in hospital. To match his large bulk he had a loud voice, which seemed to make staff turn up the volume in return when in addressing him.

As Hamlet said: *'What a piece of work is a man.'*

'But have they found my red teeshirt? I wouldn't let them cut it off me in the ambulance.'

'Where's your lost property desk? I need it, I want it back. I need it.'

'We've really done everything that we can, Andrew, but we've run into problems at this time. It's good that you're not smoking now, but the forty years of cigarettes have not done you any favours, and losing weight would help.'

'I am allergic to co-codamol and pickles. I lost five stone last year. I was 150 something kilos. Who will know where my teeshirt is? And the shower, it's crap. I've got a rain shower at home. I had an upgrade of my ensuite for 5K last year.'

'We can't put a stent in. We broke up the clot that caused your heart attack, but there is of too much silting up for a stent to be practicable. You could perhaps think about your diet too.'

'It's electrical signals that makes muscles work. I know because I work in energy. It's red. My t-shirt. You can't buy them in England. I have to go to New York for them. I go over to the States every year. When will there be someone in the lost property?'

How noble in reason ...

'I am a green energy consultant for five days a week and a DJ at weekends. I want to be out of here by Friday. I do a DJ gig at Bulwell on Saturdays. All good stuff. Seventies and Eighties, nothing after 1990. I still have heard nothing about my shirt, genuine Polo it was, not a knock-off.'

'This telly. it's ridiculous. Nine quid a day for three channels. Why can't you get Freeview? Technology has not moved on in here.'

How infinite in faculties ...

'I don't know what you make the mattresses from. Granite, I suppose. I can't sleep on it, not with my hip. I've got something a bit special at home. Cost me two grand, but worth it with my hip trouble and my lower-back pain.'

In form and moving how express and admirable …

'I'm not going till I get my teeshirt back. I like designer gear but I always go to the States for it. Take my two perfect Gucci leather jackets, £3800 and £1200 over there. You pay half as much again for seconds in the clearance malls here.'

In action how like an angel …

'Don't even think about it mate. Range-Rover's crap. Get a Toyota. Mine's a three and half litre Porsche. I had thought about a sports RR., but you could get a two litre Toyota.'

In apprehension how like a god!

'God knows when they are going to find my red teeshirt. I spend at least £150 on a pair of shoes.'

The beauty of the world …

'Where's my teeshirt? I made sure I had it when I came in here, I wouldn't let them cut it off in the ambulance.'

The paragon of animals …

'That's income lost if I'm not DJing on Saturday. And where's my fuckin' teeshirt, I'm not going without it.'

And yet to me, what is this quintessence of dust?

Robbie Dewa

War Librarian

She left a space on the shelf
in the History section
between two books
no-one ever read. She was

a miracle of efficiency
so nobody would suppose that
she had done it by accident.
Sometimes a careless browser

would move the books, so that
the small dark gap
was filled; but by the next
day's shift she had opened it

up again. She never spoke
of what had happened, and no one
ever saw her weep; but as she
stamped, and shelved, and

smiled Good Morning, she would look
across at the narrow space
between the tight close band of spines
as if she read the words

that she had lost for good; and
at the war's end she shut
the oak door on the dark day
when the news came.

The Library Man

In the end you will not hear his words;
just a thin black voice scratching
the page, like a mouse on floorboards,
the faint soft rasp of wasp-jaws
stripping varnish from a newly
painted fence. Outside the open
window, a dunnock scolds in a jingle
of small change, a blackbird tunes
into the still bell of sky. Further away
a hammered note of G, as somewhere
in the distance a yellow flashing vehicle
lays a hiss of tarmac, dulls down
the chicken-squeal of engine-voices.
And closest, private to the ear as sea
in shell, his whispered 'sssh' ; spreading
a smooth tide of quiet through the room,
lapping gently at the wall of words.

Lizzie Dunford

In Defence of Tray Bakes

You can warm cold fingers on a mug of Belfast brew
as you watch through steamed up windows
rain pelting down on the promenade.
On the counter sit rectangles of Rocky Road
lumpy with marshmallow,
Millionaire's Shortbread oozing caramel,
Chocolate Mint Slices, Malteser Squares,
Jammy Joeys in coconut coats,
Fifteens, sliced like salami
but sticky with glace cherries,
thick with condensed milk.

The name's misleading.
No real baking involved, just assembling ingredients.
You can go upmarket, buy posh versions
with pistachios and expensive chocolate
in dainty paper cases,
but when the weather's Baltic
and you're feeling foundered
you need a decent sized slab of something sweet
to gladden the damp grey world.

Entertaining Angels

It was Friday, and Amanda had come round after school for tea. At 4 pm, there was a loud ring on the doorbell, and there was James Charles O'Neill.

Mum used to say you could set the clock by him. Every day, after lunch at the Cripples Institute, he tramped into town to buy the *Irish Times,* then called with us on his way home for a cup of tea and two biscuits. Or two scones, or two pieces of shortbread or apple tart if Mum had been baking. Always two – and two spoonfuls of sugar in his tea.

'You're spoiling me, you're spoiling me! What would my father and mother say?'

He would say this every time, then tuck in. Crumbs all down his chin. He slurped his tea, made clicking sounds with his loose false teeth. His clothes stank of pipe smoke – he always wore baggy mole-brown corduroys, a waistcoat and hairy tweed jacket. And his Trinity tie, of course – spattered with food stains. After tea, he would fish in his pocket for matches and his tin of Mick McQuaid, fiddle about with pipe cleaners, then tamp down the tobacco, sputter, puff, and settle down read the news. At 4.45, he would fold the paper, heave himself out of the armchair, thank my mother profusely, and shuffle off – until the next day.

Mum said it was a pity of him, he'd been a brilliant young man though he was a little bit different, and that we should be kind, we should always welcome strangers, you might be entertaining angels unaware.

He was different all right. At church he always sat in the front row and snored like a pig until it was time for the Lord's Prayer, when he would shuffle to his feet and roar out 'OurFatherWhoArtInHeaven' in a carrying baritone, racing to reach a loud Amen before the rest of the congregation.

But at church, at least, I could pretend not to know him.

It wasn't usually a problem if Mr O'Neill coincided with Amanda – I would make sure we were out on our bikes or upstairs in my bedroom if it was raining. Today, however, my mother was at a meeting and had instructed me to look after James Charles.

I wanted to be Amanda. She had the longest, blondest hair in the class and was always picked first for rounders. Today, she looked beautiful in her bell-bottom trousers and pastel tank top: she never had to wear hand-me-downs from her cousins. She certainly didn't have weirdos visiting the redbrick villa with white carpets and immaculate furniture where she lived with her tennis playing mother and father.

Amanda's eyes glittered with curiosity as James Charles shuffled in, bidding us good afternoon, and settled himself in his usual chair in the living room. He seemed to be even smellier than usual. I hurried Amanda into the adjoining kitchen while I warmed the teapot, but she kept peering through the door at Mr O'Neill.

'Is he mental? Why does he come to your house, anyway? He really stinks, doesn't he? Is that a Republican paper? My Dad gets the Belfast Telegraph, he says he wouldn't touch a paper from the South of Ireland.'

Amanda was flushed with excitement. There was no point trying to distract her with chocolate digestives.

'Yes, he's completely mental. He comes from Dublin, that's why he reads that paper. He comes every bloody day. Even Christmas Day. He always says the same things, every single day – 'Only two spoonfuls of sugar, please', 'You're spoiling me, you're spoiling me, what would my father and mother say?' He comes every day at 4 o'clock. He's stinky and annoying and I'm fed up with it.'

'I don't blame you. Amanda's eyes were bright with mischief. I know, why don't we play a trick on him? See if he even notices! Where do you keep the salt?'

We were shaking with repressed laughter as Mr O'Neill selected his two biscuits – *You're spoiling me, you're spoiling me.* We hid in the kitchen to watch him sip the tea, giggling as he wrinkled his nose, shook his head a little in puzzlement, then drank it down regardless, wincing.

'That was so funny!' said Amanda. I said I thought it was hilarious, but I was beginning to dread my mother's return. In fact, she was late and preoccupied with parish matters and forgot to inquire about James Charles' visit.

*****

The next day was Saturday and sunny. My younger brothers were doing circuits of the garden on their trikes; I was sitting on the swing, sucking toffees and trying to read my library book while keeping an eye on the front gate. I kept checking my watch.

Four o'clock: no Mr O'Neill. I waited till five o'clock, although the sun had disappeared behind clouds and it was quite chilly. I felt sick.

My mother remarked upon the unaccustomed absence. 'Was Mr O'Neill his usual self yesterday? You looked after him all right, didn't you?'

I muttered something and was grateful when my brothers distracted her, squabbling over their Matchbox cars. That night, I couldn't sleep. What if Mr O'Neill were really ill? What if we'd poisoned him? What if he died? When I finally succumbed to sleep, I dreamed I was sprinkling salt on slugs which writhed in agony and gazed at me with a puzzled expression on their brownish faces.

*****

Church on Sunday morning was torture. *Truly I tell you, whatever you did for one of the least of my brethren, you did unto me* was the text for my father's sermon. I glimpsed Amanda across the aisle. She was wearing a new dress in white broderie anglaise with matching patent shoes and her blonde hair had been curled in ringlets. A beam of sunlight filtered through the stained glass and created a halo effect around her head as she gazed ahead, apparently rapt in meditation. *Forgive us our trespasses and deliver us from evil.* No Mr O'Neill in the front row to race to the last Amen. After the service, I avoided Amanda and made an effort to talk to wee Mr McCoubrey, who had been invited to join us for Sunday lunch.

The afternoon crawled by. It was sunny again and my wee brothers were playing with water pistols in the front garden, peering over the fence and shooting passing traffic. I was perched in a deckchair, library book unopened on my knee, trying to acquire a tan and to avoid checking my watch. Four o'clock.

Suddenly the boys began to yell, 'Look, look! Look at that car! It must be a Jaguar! Or a Rolls Royce!'

I ran to the fence, where a very large, shiny limousine was purring to a halt in front of the Manse. A man in a peaked cap got out and hurried round to open the front passenger door. A very elegant woman in a pale blue dress and matching hat emerged. The driver now opened the back door of the car to reveal – James Charles O'Neill, in a darkish suit, still wearing his Trinity tie.

I rushed around the side of the house and hid behind a holly bush. I could hear the clip clopping of the lady's high heels and the loud ring of the doorbell.

'Good afternoon, you must be the minister's wife. I'm James Charles' sister, just up from Ballsbridge for the weekend – we took him to the Crawfordsburn Inn for tea yesterday and we've just been to the Culloden for lunch. James Charles has been telling me how kind you all are. Just a little token of our gratitude. No thank you, we won't come in, we must be on our way.'

I remained hidden until I heard the big car pull away and I judged it safe to go inside, where my brothers were playing with their Matchbox cars and my mother was arranging an enormous bouquet of expensive looking flowers and muttering to herself.

'Crawfordsburn Inn, indeed! Culloden Hotel! It'd be a sight better if they took him home to Dublin. Suppose he wouldn't fit in to their smart dinner parties.'

Mum slammed the vase down on the piano and hurried off to make sandwiches for the Presbyterian Women's Bible Study Group. Suddenly, I felt grateful that she was my mother, even if she didn't play tennis or wear scarlet nail polish. Perhaps she was entertaining angels, unaware.

I think, nowadays, James Charles O'Neill would be diagnosed on the autistic spectrum, albeit very high functioning.

Guitar

On your right hand, the nails are long, strong ovals;
on the left, clipped short. Your fingertips
are leather-tough, unlike the rest of you,
flicking that flop of fair fringe from pale blue eyes,
soft-voiced, hesitant, blurry-edged
in your oatmeal jersey, faded flares
and that fusty Afghan coat you wear inside
the bedsit, where condensation drips
down windowpanes and you've wedged
old copies of the *Guardian* under doors
to stop the draughts.

You reach for your guitar.
Honey-amber light spills from cedar-wood;
damp walls of mildew green speckled with mould
recede, and as you pluck the strings
I feel the sun's rays on my skin,
breathe heavy scent of orange blossom.
I glimpse a scarlet riot of geraniums,
purple bougainvillea rampages on terracotta roofs.
Lizards bask in the heat. On a rickety table,
a jug of wine, saucers of salty almonds,
fat green olives. I stretch numb fingers
in the strum of sunlight,
inhale chords, devour vibrations,
and for the time it takes to play *Aranjuez*
you flame, dark-sparking eyes, coal-black hair,
fiery as a flamenco dancer.

Sue Gale

The Spanish Armada

Maggie Dempsey stood very still. Staring through a classroom window smeared with a thousand finger marks, her tears threatened to overflow onto her cheeks. Oblivious to the devastating afternoon their teacher had had, a few boys from her class were kicking a ball around on the shimmering asphalt but she did not see them.

The lesson she had organised so carefully had not gone to plan. Afterwards, the inspector's words had stung her so severely she doubted she would ever forget them.

Forty-five minutes before (was it only forty-five minutes?), she had retrieved lost trainers and grubby sweatshirts for the usual culprits and the children had filed noisily out of the room. Then she seated herself awkwardly on a child's chair opposite the inspector at the front of the class. The inspector stared at her notes for some time before looking up.

'Now Miss Dempsey. Your lesson today - the Spanish Armada. You say,' she paused to look at her notes again. 'You say you wanted the children to understand what the Armada was, and what it looked like when it arrived. But....' She looked straight into Maggie's face.

'There is no evidence that that is what they learned. And there are no precise learning goals for the children, according to their ability.'

She raised her eyebrows, and her lips attempted a stiff little smile.

'Well, no,' said Maggie weakly. 'I like them to work together and learn from each other.' She stopped. The inspector was scribbling something down and did not appear to be listening.

'And anyway,' she ploughed on. 'It was so hot out there today. When they came back after play, it seemed a bit, well, heavy going. Who wants to talk about the Spanish Armada on the hottest day of the year?'

Maggie laughed with nervous hilarity, but the inspector's face suggested she had made a grave error. The laptop screen became an even greater barrier between them.

'Are you planning to continue this topic at another time? It's part of the curriculum for this group. You'll need to teach it before the end of term, and time marches on...' She smiled thinly but did not bother to look at Maggie when she said this. Maggie was silent. She looked around the room at the colourful displays, the half-finished models and the paint trays which had not yet been cleared away. She felt she was sinking further and further down. Miserably she fiddled with her pen.

'OK.' The inspector sighed in an all-is-not-lost kind of way. 'Let's look at what the children *did* learn today. Can you tell me more about what was going on in the Book Corner?'

Maggie leant forward. She was on safer ground now. With more enthusiasm she said: 'That was a rehearsal for a play about the Great Plague. Gillian's written it herself at home. I want to encourage this kind of thing and…'

The inspector glared at Maggie who was suddenly aware of the patches of chalk dust on the front of her cardigan.

'But it was very noisy,' the inspector said, 'and some of the final death throes were rather agonising and prolonged. The other children were clearly distracted by what was going on and I was unsure how this linked with the whole Spanish Armada theme. I noticed you didn't intervene. Why was that?'

Maggie felt defensive, but at the same time she was aware of the danger any attack may provoke.

'That was deliberate. They were being very imaginative…'

The inspector interrupted her, 'True - but what were they actually learning? And why did you allow that child to fall asleep on her desk at the back? Did you even notice her?'

Maggie felt the stirrings of anger at the back of her throat. Poor little Jeanette. Living in a hotel room with her mother and two younger siblings did not allow for much sleep.

'Of course I noticed her,' she said as sharply as she dared. 'She has some personal issues. This is a safe place for her.'

There was an awkward silence as the inspector made more notes. Maggie laced her fingers together tightly and fidgeted on her chair.

'Right,' the inspector said. 'And what exactly was happening with the little group you were sitting with? It sounded like a very heated exchange about a football game?'

'Well, it was really,' said Maggie knowing all was lost now. 'I was trying to draw parallels between the Forest game last night against Swindon, and the Spanish Armada, you know Spain versus England.' Her voice dropped to a whisper. 'I admit it wasn't very successful. They only wanted to talk about the football after that.'

The inspector stared back at her.

'But there is some maths there.' Maggie revived a little and continued recklessly. 'We keep a record of the scores every week, averages and so on...' Her voice trailed away. The inspector glanced up with feigned incredulity.

'Football. Not precisely what springs to mind when teaching about the Spanish Armada.' She adjusted her laptop. Miserably Maggie stared out of the window.

'Now – Aidan, is it? I tried speaking to him while he was drawing but he wouldn't talk to me at all. Wouldn't even look at me.'

'Adrian. He's a selective mute,' said Maggie. The inspector tapped her pen accusingly on Maggie's lesson notes.

'Not mentioned in your plan Miss Dempsey. You must include how you are catering for every single child in the class particularly those with special needs.'

Maggie thought of the hours she had spent with Adrian, talking quietly and encouraging him. She could hardly trust herself to speak.

'But they've all got special needs,' she said at last. 'Some paint well, some can't hold a tune, some can't hop on the spot ten times to save their lives…'

The inspector was impatient.

'I think you know what I mean, Miss Dempsey. There should be detailed learning goals for all these children and,' she looked down at her notes. 'They don't seem to be here.'

Maggie felt everything sliding away from her. She was under attack, out of her depth and the waters were closing in over her head. She breathed in deeply.

'I know these children very well,' she said more loudly than she had intended. 'I have been teaching most of them for nearly two years. I know their parents. I know their strengths and weaknesses, their little foibles. I know how they learn. I don't need a plan for every single one of them…'

'Nevertheless…' The inspector looked away having attempted to soften the expression on her face. She closed her notebook and the laptop.

'I'm sorry Miss Dempsey. I have been hard pressed to find evidence of any learning going on at all and…'

'You're failing me.' Maggie's voice was flat and without emotion.

'Not you personally, Miss Dempsey. Just your lesson.' The inspector placed some notes on the table.

'Look through these and I'll come and see you again in a month's time.' She stood and leant forward to shake Maggie's hand, but she was already making her way to the window so that the inspector could not see the tears in her eyes.

So, this is the support I was promised? she thought. Rather than the patronising insults she had endured, she would have preferred a scathing 'this lesson was rubbish' and they could both have gone their own ways. Shame and anger rose within her. Shame that she had found herself in this situation again. Anger that the inspector had made no allowances for the children, exhausted after playtime under the blistering sun, arriving back in the classroom sweating and irritable. Unsurprisingly, they had not been receptive to Maggie's description of Francis Drake watching the arrival of the Spanish, and her energetic mime of playing bowls. Then, in some desperation, she had asked them to imagine they were sailors on the Armada. What did they see? How did they feel? But she knew all they could see was the clock ticking away slowly on the wall, and all they could feel was anticipation that the end of the day and freedom were not far away.

The inspector's notes lay like an unexploded bomb in the middle of Maggie's desk. She ignored them and began to read the writing the children had produced. In that hot, empty room her heart sank even lower. Some had tried to re-write the story, but their work was untidy, factually incorrect, and illustrated with drawings of German U-boats and cabin cruisers. Others had managed a jumble of short unpunctuated sentences. She wondered why she had spent a whole afternoon last week teaching them about capital letters, full stops and the use of the apostrophe.

She could bear it no longer and stuffed the rest of the books into her bag. Another night marking with a microwaved lasagne in front of Netflix.

She walked towards the door and saw a sheet of paper lying under a desk. Adrian. Of course. He neither spoke, read out loud nor wrote, but produced beautiful detailed drawings as if all the skills he did not have, had been rolled into the one enormous talent he did possess. She turned the sheet over and found a drawing of a Spanish galleon, the texture of the wood picked out in differentiated pencil strokes, the sails billowing out behind in the wind. It was a brilliant piece of work. She would pin it up on the wall tomorrow.

As she looked more carefully, she saw a stick man leaning over the edge of the galleon with a speech bubble coming out of his mouth. This contained the first words she had ever known Adrian to write.

'Ahoy ther u inglis barsteds.'

Not an entirely unsuccessful day then.

Janet Gibson

A Salutary Tale

Mother did warn me, often as she rocked me in her scale covered arms, whilst we reposed in our den. How comfortable we were, we two, quiet, peaceful, whilst Dad was out on the rampage. She would croon her words of wisdom which dwelt in my heart. I hoped never to forget these nuggets of information. Our kind are known for having long memories of the Past.

I went outside to play in the long grass, scorched lands surrounding us. I never realised why, the penny never dropped, as human kind might say.

One day, still only a juvenile, I laughed, but instead of a giggle I breathed fire and brimstone. Such a funny taste in my mouth afterwards.

I ran indoors crying hot tears and Mater said 'Oh darling! I did tell you this may happen as you start to grow older.'

'It hurts and is nasty and I might injure someone by accident', I replied.

'No danger sweetie, we just learn by experience; when opening our mouths, we may cause this outcome. Just think calm thoughts and keep your mouth closed. A silent dragon is a safe dragon.'

Just a Drop

I am like a diamond, pure, clear,
I glisten, catch the sun,
I splash,
I gather in puddles,
I flow,
I glide,
I can rush down mountain sides,
I create lakes,
I make streams and rivers,
I am needed for those who populate earth,
I quench thirst,
I water crops, trees, flowers.

A Gardener's Compendium

Seed shaker
Hoe hurrier
Spade stepper
Rake racer
Shear swisher
Dobber dabbler
Weed worrier
Soil sifter
Grass guzzler
Can carrier

Barry Harper

Brave *Action Men*

Two boys playing with twin *Action Man* toys
One's a courageous deep sea diver
Grey 'goldfish bowl' helmet and heavy boots
The other's a fearless astronaut
NASA suit and large space capsule
Silver dog tags swing on chiselled chests
Stark reminder never mix them up

But even macho soldiers can suffer stress
When combatting shock of a mother's death
Young conscripts fighting what they can't see
Shell-shock battle fatigue and trauma
From which they may never recover
Fortunately they are God's gift to each other
Without which they couldn't have battled through

Playing quietly, naive heads spinning
On their perished elastic necks
The bond is ocean deep, no space for words
They can't speak for they are plastic
and are treated as such
If you pull their cords they will say the same
Emotionless words over and again

Now each understands how it feels
Never to be allowed to cry
Even action heroes need space for
Love and the occasional tender hug
But no one will talk to them and

They don't know how to ask for help
To relieve the pressure cooker
In their chaotic heads

Even the twin boys can't come to terms
With what's befallen their brave new toys

I Come From…

I come from
soot soaked bricks,
the bitter smell of coal fires
and the drone of
Rolls Royce Merlin engines
from smashed panes
and broken buildings
from dirty pavements
and dusty dreams
from honest working folk
toiling hard to
eek out good money
I come from church school
with cane and slipper
I sometimes deserved
I am from a place where
I'm proud to belong
but desire to be different
the consequence of being
an identical twin
I come from

Origin of the Species
and Frozen Planet
from belief in ozone
not a depleted coal seam
I come from 'Ay up me duck'
and generations of miners
from a town with
a headstock but no pits
I come from breaking up fights
and walking damp streets
from saxophones and violin
but not from a place
where people can sing
I come from a greenhouse
growing dahlias like my dad
mending socks without moaning
just like my mum
I'm now from
central heating
but can still
smell the smog
of a roaring fire
being drawn
by a stretched
Daily Sketch
I never read...

Rocky Horror Show

I am the apex predator
Top dog in my saline world
If you mess with me I will eat you
I'm the only carnivorous gastropod
And I'm feared by my feeble prey
Like a polar bear tracking on ice
Or a tiger pouncing in the jungle
I stalk damp rocks at low tide
Hunting for seaside snacks
They try to flee when they sense me
But I'm much quicker than they are
Okay it may take me a day
To complete the hundred millimetre dash
But in my universe that's lightening fast
During my thirteen year lifespan
I'll commute no more than thirty metres
Carrying a sea view airbnb on my back
But when I move for sure they'll know it
Just follow my trail of shell devastation
I am the World renowned Atlantic dog whelk
Or should I say Nucella lapillus
A grey shelled giant four centimetres large
Current legend in my own rock pool
Ambushing unsuspecting victims
They are a veritable seafood smorgasbord
Wave after wave of gastronomic gastropods
Mussels cockles oysters and barnacles
I might even resort to cannibalism
If the selfish shellfish get in my way
I Gracefully glide on my slimy mucus film
Clamber over them with a muscular foot
Bore through their pathetic shells

With my rapid rasping proboscis
Injecting their insides with chemicals
Acidic enzymes turn flesh into rich soup
Sucking up a bouillabaisse banquet
However scraping up a meal
Can take seventy-two hours
But this is genuine fast food take-away
Salty full of calories with free drink
And I'll shell out an arm and a leg
But It'll tide me over for a few more days

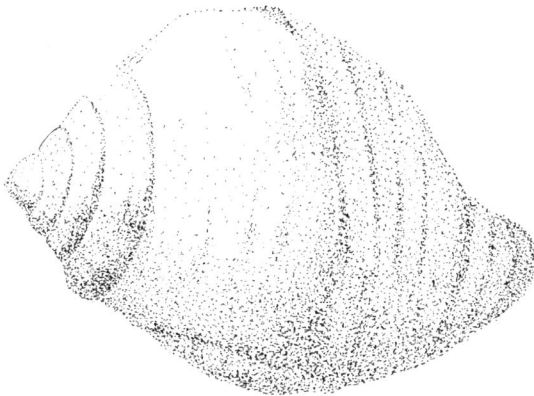

Dog Whelk (Nucella lapillus)

Julia Hodson

Orvieto Cathedral

Orvieto Cathedral was described by Pope Urban the Sixth as 'divine'. Now I can argue with any Pope about lots of things but on this particular point the Pontiff was right!

The facade of the Cathedral stands head and shoulders above everything in the vicinity and is visible from miles away, but as the inappropriately dressed tourists scramble up the steep medieval streets it becomes impossible to see it until you locate the Piazza del Duomo, not that it has a dome actually.

Naturally the Brits of a certain demographic have stupidly arrived in the early afternoon to find the Tourist Information Centre closed, the shops shut and the waiters tired from the lunch service and girding their loins for the evening ahead.

Throngs of teenagers on day trips from schools criss cross the piazza with the more leisured flaneur. A busker asks the kids to quieten down as his singing and strumming cannot be heard above their racket. There is silence for a moment and he strikes up a new tune. After a few bars the young ones serenade him - all together now.

Local Italians go about their daily business and you can listen in to see if you can recognise any of the 'online' Italian phrases that have prepared you for this visit. The only three words that I could make out were: 'ciao', 'preggo' and 'mangare'.

There is much oo-ing and arr-ing as the Cathedral comes into view. A neck-aching, back-breaking spectacle of intricate carving, sculpture, statuary, bronze figures, gilding, brightly coloured mosaics. Not a centimetre is free of decoration of the highest quality. It draws you in again and again to focus on the detail in absolute wonder. The narrative of Christ from the Annunciation to Final Judgement.

You have to stand with your back against the perimeter buildings of the Piazza to fit the massive frontage within the frame of your camera lens. More proximate to the building are the youth of today pouting into their phones with the soon to be forgotten backdrop of the Madonna and Child looking down on them with a bemused beatific gaze.

From the East Door comes a group of young, pale grey and white clad Chinese nuns. Enjoying themselves with an abandon unexpected of women of the cloth, well not since Julie Andrews found that the Austrian hills were alive.

Relief is sought in cafe bar on the square, taking a moment to practice the words, 'Serra, due cappuccino per favor.' Only to receive the reply, 'two coffees with milk. Anything to eat? Due gelato will follow, the local hazelnut flavour, these will be delicious. Duly watered and fed instinctively you will realise it's time to work the shops and meander down hill back to your Fiat 500 hire car and head off to Bolsena. That's where it all started with the priest who doubted the transubstantiation of the bread and wine hundreds of years ago.

Thankfully the tourist memorabilia maintains a fairly high standard of good taste, just the one T shirt lowering the tone by carrying in English the words, 'HOME IS WHERE WIFI CONNECTS AUTOMATICALLY'.

Eyeing a potential purchase of a ceramic olive oil and balsamic vinegar vessel, a young Chinese nun - a little on the stocky side I thought - plonked herself between me and the object of my desire. She struck an unreligious pose and one of her Sisters took a photo of her in front of the shop display. 'Ciao, preggo, mangare,' she shouted and was gone!

1984 Revisited

The bomb blast shook the building. Some lesser mortals were removed by firemen and ferried to hospital. Seagulls and sirens still screeched outside. There was a man in a white coat shining a very bright torch into my eyes. He was giving me instructions in a soft authoritative voice.

'Look up….look down…look right… and finally… look left.'

Inexplicably I said, 'this lady's not for turning.'

That's when I noticed the other people. A rare collection of oddities standing behind the man and looking at me. I was sitting on the end of a four poster bed. I clutched my blue velour dressing gown closer. In the opposite corner a man in a smoking jacket was practising putting a golf ball.

'Do you know where you are?' the man with the torch asked.

'If you are a doctor … then I am in a hospital. And if not, then why are all these people in my hotel bedroom?' I gave them a hard stare and they shuffled uncomfortably.

'What year is it?' he probed. What a strange question. I heard someone whisper 'George Orwell'.

Just then I spotted a uniformed police constable in the gaggle and so I replied, humorously, or so I thought, 'Animal Farm.' The ensemble shook their heads. 'No coaching,' cautioned the doctor.

'Who are you?' he asked. Well, the audacity of the man.

A woman in a suit, held up a hat and a handbag, and gesticulated behind the doctor that they were mine. Obviously I was The Queen. I gave a condescending shake of my head and raised my chin regally. I remained silent.

An older, sleep-weary man approached us. 'Look Doc,' he said with an air of desperation, 'She looks ok.'

'Less of the "she" I am not the cat's mother,' I interjected.

He carried on, 'she looks ok. A bit dishevelled but that's not a problem. We need her to be seen. Inspire public confidence. Let's get her on the balcony. She can wave to the press. A few pics and then you can carry on.'

The doctor shook his head.

'Well give her that word association test. Let's get this thing done with,' pleaded the man. Unusually I felt quite sorry for him.

'I'm going to say a word', said the doctor, 'and I want you to respond with the first word that comes to mind.'

I nodded royal assent. I love being tested. I was hoping for anagrams. He started rather quickly…

'Number 10', he asserted.

'That's two words,' I replied. His questions and my answers came quickly after that:

Q. Cabinet?	A. Chippendale.
Q. Men?	A. Chippendales.
Q. Coal?	A. Strike.
Q. Falklands?	A. Victory.
Q. Battle?	A. Orgreave.
Q. President?	A. Good looking chap. Whatshisname?

Q. Grantham?	A. Where?
Q. Chemistry?	A. Oxford.
Q. Iron?	A. Lady!

From the look on their faces my little crowd of supporters was evidently going through a roller coaster of emotions. The telephone in the room rang suddenly and they all jumped in a kind of unified startle response. The smoking jacket man picked up the receiver.

We waited for him to speak. Solemnly he told us, 'That was Her Majesty the Queen, ringing to offer her condolences on the death of your…'

I stood up immediately and held my hand out to stop him mid flow. For then I knew who I was and what this circus was all about.

I said confidently to the handbag woman, 'fetch my pink Chanel suit this instant.' Her mouth dropped open, and I continued.

'I know you would like to have it cleaned to remove the blood. But no, I will wear it with conviction and let the world see what they have done. For I am none other than Jaqueline Bouvier Kennedy. And I will survive.'

The doctor looked at the police officer. 'Officer, I'm afraid that you will have to exercise your powers under Section 136 of the Mental Health Act.' The policeman put on his hat and stepped forward. "She'll need to be in a public place for that.' I heard him say.

'Dennis,' the doctor said, ' will you escort Mrs Thatcher outside. Preferably via the tradesman's entrance.'

Cafe Culture

A sonnet for our times

Stand back I'm on a mission for coffee
Long queue blocked by indecisive choosers
Steaming hot froth over treacly toffee
Full on breakfasts for the weary boozers
Lonely couples empty nest controllers
Loud business bores avoid office stresses
Pram confined crawlers Sunday lunch spoilers
Pub pulls now grim gals in last nights dresses
Phone and lap top tappers, selfies posted
Outside smokers succumb to their vices
A carbon footprint locally roasted
Third world fair trade but now first world prices
Ink skinned blank eyed baristas set the vibe
I look around and see this is my tribe.

Lindah Kiddey

The Wager

The greyhound strode along the winding driveway of raked sand and gravel, gaining distance from the Manor. This was no ordinary dog. It could have stepped from a classic Stubbs painting, leaving a lonesome thoroughbred stallion tethered for eternity within the canvas. A beautiful hound, its coat a dappled fine silver grey with a darker saddle patch across its strong, muscular back. When at rest, its long, tapered forelegs stretched out delicately to reveal the sheen of black paws and lustrous ebony claws. Now, its tail was alert, signalling to left and right as it trotted; graceful, determined, purposeful, powerful. The dog's liquorice-dark eyes shone bright. He wore a collar of finest burgundy leather from which hung an oval silver disk. It turned with every movement just below its chiseled muzzle and bore his name, Bonaparte.

Nobody was in sight. An early morning mist competed with shafts of apricot dawn light. The hound moved through the coastal parkland, its fine head, arched neck and lower legs lost in and out of vision, its lean trunk randomly disappearing into the lingering sea fret. A phantom dog? No, this dog was very present. It stopped and stood, quiet and solid as stone. Suddenly its ears rose sharply, articulating like two small, pointed land sails testing the wind.

Jack Fawcett lay on his back, motionless. Thick red hair, viciously wrenched from its sodden neck-bow during the conflict, made delta-like patterns across his pale, sweated complexion.

A crust of dark, congealed blood blocked one nostril, the full, dry, split lips slightly parted showed cream solid teeth and pink spittle. His thick russet lashes closed over a bulging, blackened socket. Steam rose as he breathed shallowly into the crisp dew. A long, low groan emerged as his good eye slowly opened.

The contest had been gentlemanly. They had argued then agreed a price, a time, a place and a plan were set. It would be a bare-knuckle test of strength with no need for seconds or indeed any witnesses. This was between them both alone. The wager was settled. To the winner, a purse of gold and the racing hound of pure lineage now destined for stud, a fine, fitting retirement for such a beast. He had been trained from a pup for the race, the chase and the finish which he had won on countless occasions, his name well known to the wider fraternity of wealthy gamblers and chancers. He, Bonaparte, would have his pick of eager pedigree bitches, endless gnawing bones, and a rugged blanket set between burnished fire grates before the open hearth as even colder evenings drew in. And, for his master, a handsome breeder's income and envied reputation.

The dog sat tensed, spine rigid, eyes fixed on a distant point. It rose silently, four legs planted and ready. It ran, and what a run. Limbs stretched, powered shoulders, paws meeting in quartet at each giant stride. It cleared the park into the mossy woodland, nose raised to take in the scent of fungal soil and leaf mould as it followed a different, distant scent, and sound.

Fawcett, rose slowly and coughed, elbows and knees dimpling the wet grass. Casting aside a heavy woollen cover he did not recognise, he looked about him. His whole body ached but he was whole. Tentative fingers located a puffed and deeply cut nose; a soil-filled ear; a purple, bulbous slit of an eye; a wincingly tender chin; protesting ribs; his best breeches beyond repair, and a missing boot. He sat and then, turning stiffly saw a glint of silver emerging from the dark spinney.

Bonaparte raced towards him like cannon shot, then slowed sharply. He trotted forward then stood, balancing on his hind legs, keeping a distance as if sensing the man's injuries. Fawcett raised one knee on which he pressed down hard to rise, somewhat giddily to his full height. They moved towards each other. With paws and hands rested on each other's shoulder the vanquished fighter and hound embraced. This dog and this master would surely never be parted.

Merton-Johns, the victor, lay with one naked foot to the fire, the other cast sideways, burrowed deep into the weave of a thick Berber rug. To his side stood an empty silver claret jug, its surface reflecting the diminishing embers glowing beyond. A crystal goblet rocked lazily on the waxed and knotted oak floor. He turned, belched, and gasped at a stabbing pain. His fists were bruised and grazed, his jaw rough and reddened, his groin pinched and burned as he settled a hip. His ear was torn, smeared with dried blood. The ripped silk shirt he wore was stained with clay and speckled with gore. He wondered if it was his own or Fawcett's as he pushed back a muddy cuff, brown and limp. Looking about the panelled room he slowly gathered his thoughts. He had won, but where was his hound?

He could recall looping his belt through its collar and its eyes glancing between him and his master who lay still and silent where he had fallen. The cloak he had cast over the unconscious man would have protected him from the autumn chill. He bore him no ill, certainly not a cold, undeserved death. Merton rose slowly and sat, cracked fingernails kneading his rattled, pulsing skull through grubby curls.

He tried to recall his return homeward after the contest. He and the beast had entered the Hall, of that he was certain. He also recalled rowdily toasting his success again and again with an excess of a fine vintage, then all was blank.

A second belch brought forth a taste of bile which burned his chops and made him retch. Then a series of sighs and a torrent of sound, an angry, roaring wrath, of irritation and frustration, a troubled pause and the quiet of acceptance. The dog was gone. That fine animal would surely have sought out his true master who had reared him, trained, cared for and loved him as a fond companion, a champion, a brother. An unwelcome truth was due. The gold was his, the fight was his, but the greyhound, Bonaparte, never.

Guy Kiddey

Don't Wear White

Cloying, sultry, like a sauna without steam, the white-hot sun glares at the sturdy raised veg beds. Plants are rich green, well-watered and fed, surrounded by what was once lawn, now the colour of dusty lions, of dried corn-dollies in a village garden.

And here is a woman: white designer t-shirt and shorts, white flip-flops, white shades, and white sun hat on white canvas lounger. The sky is a blue arc with no end. Her eyes squint, even behind UV lenses. Pages turn lazily.

A small brown stain appears, unnoticed on a pristine sleeve. A winged insect 'let's one go' mid-flight. An aerial easy turn and a 'couldn't care less' moment of oozing release.

Manic, crowded bush tomatoes squat in their grow bags, a sea of yellow pixy-hatted flowers with tough, determined fruits multiplying, it seems, by the hour. One expensively manicured foot rests, toes splayed in vain hope of a cooling breeze. No chance on this climate-defying Autumn Saturday. Where oh where are those dirty violet rain-carrying clouds?

And here they come … ants. Not in large number, but scurrying, bouldering across uneven terrain. Not a second thought. 'Feastings ahead lads, go for it.' Tender glistening skin shiny with sun bloc and sweat, a white strap the perfect landmark for micro scouts on reconnaissance, evil mandibles at the ready. God, what a feast. Little bastards nip, some die under the flailing sole and yells of protest from the sunbather, others just leg it for now, determined on another assault. The gold-edged heels of white sandals now sport a pale brown dust margin which does nothing for their elegance, and two small bite dots rise, red and puffy to the surface of a waxed leg.

And here, evolution in full view.

Two ground-feeding blackbirds swinging on a sunflower? Not just jumping and pecking but lunging and hanging with determined, crazy acrobatics, dark wings flapping, claws grasping, picking out dainty delights for the brood. The sun turns their feathers into jagged fans. 'We will feed anywhere' they tweet.

An unseen guano parcel drops silently, strategically onto the edge of the canvas chair, just as the white t-shirted body leans forward then relaxes back. A deft greenish bull's eye. And the sun beats down to dry up the dropping and fix it securely to the Egyptian cotton.

A delicate splash from above. A pale-yellow stain on the short's crotch. A mystery. Do birds piss-poo in flight too? Does anything and everything piss-poo in flight? Marathon runners widdle as they thunder along the roads and by-ways, so do birds and butterflies and all flying things find guiltless relief en route to wherever?

And then a gobbet of wet from above the far hedge. Next Door's kids paddle-pooling, waving the hose and laughing, bumping, squealing, enjoying the cool in the heat, small bodies grubby with the confetti of grass, sandy-mud, dripping fruity icicles, clear snot. Their hose water is not pristine and sprays a dozen droplets that dance across the white shirted chest of their neighbour. Surely not coffee granules? More like rust, inner slime burned to the inside of the rubber, and it smells.

Then a call from the cool of the kitchen, 'Assam or Builders?' A white tea tray carrying white mugs, a slight stumble, a spoon takes flight, a strategic splash of tiffin on white sunhat. And then a chocolate drip from the dark Florentine biscuits, and then a fallen nut with a gummy crumb of crystallised fruit. Both T-shirt and missiles are equally warmed to perfection to guarantee several 'real bastard' stains.

A warning to style lovers …be careful when you wear white.

Players

They flicked marbles in flinty mill races
Where green moss met the wetness of sedges
Running fast to such dangerous places
Legs grass-painted with sore gritted knees.

Bee stings and nettle bites iodine dyed
Purple-red daubs follow rough-tumble games
Signs of inventiveness fearlessly tried
In scuffed sandals and rip-ridden socks

The farmyard apple-scrump ladder espied
By stink bomb lobbers and worm magnifiers
Kids grown smarter with wild ventures vied
And memories sparking of days well played.

They might try you and cause consternation
But these kids have grown clever with intellects sharp
Deep-delving, researching a vaccine salvation
To stamp on this plague like a fledgling bare.

Guy Kiddey

Chris Niven

The Changing Room

Beryl - Big Blue Hair - BBH

Doreen – Everything Too Tight - ETT

They work in a mill shop famous for its designer clothes at bargain prices. They are standing near the changing rooms attending to a customer whilst also sorting out stock.

BBH: It opens today you know.

ETT: I know, I can't believe there's all this fuss over a flippin' Asda opening. The Co-op never had this palaver.

BBH: 24 hour shopping too. What's all that about? Who wants to go shopping at two in the mornin'?

ETT: Perverts that's who.

BBH: You're not wrong Doreen. Normal people don't want to pursue pork pies at all hours of the night do they?

ETT: Shift workers, that's different. They might suddenly have the urge for a custard tart at 5.30. Well, you can understand that.

[Pause]

BBH: He's been seen again, you know.

ETT: He hasn't? What's she gonna do? She deserves better than him.

BBH: He's gorra a wig now. Our Ken saw him, said he looked liked a 70's porn star with his Tom Selleck moustache, a flash cream suit and a bloomin' red tinged wig.

ETT: Red tinged! His hair's mousy brown. I bet that blends in nicely. And they say men don't have a menopause.

[Pause]

BBH: Are you still on the patches?

ETT: Yeh, when I remember.

BBH: Any good?

ETT: They were ok at first, then they seemed to go off.

BBH: Oh no. Did you go back to the docs?

ETT: (Laughing) No cause I realised I was putting our Malc's nicotine patches on by mistake.

[Request from the cubicle]

BBH: [Posh voice] Yes, madam I will check to see if we have an enlarged size. I won't be a moment. Let me examine the rails.

To BBH [Whispering] Blimey, she took a 12 into the changing room, who does she think she is, Kate Moss? She's going to have to have to have liposuction to get into a 14. It's a shame really, she was always a real looker when she was younger. Always had lots of lads round her.

ETT: [Whispering] It wasn't just her good looks that attracted them Beryl. She was putting it about a bit too. They reckon her second isn't her husband's, you know. They say she had a fling with that insurance man, the door to door bloke with the flash car and the quiff. He thought he was God's gift. Seems he had a wife and baby in Ingoldmells that he conveniently forgot to mention.

BBH: I am going to do these reductions, Doreen. Then they'll be ready for the weekend.

ETT: OK. [Pause]. Did I tell you our Jaqueline is thinking of havin' a boob job?

BBH: Your J? What on earth for? She's got a lovely pair. She don't need one.

ETT: That's what I said, but she says that Liam says that it will improve her modelling chances.

BBH: Has she had any jobs lately?

ETT: Well, she had a photo shoot in Derby not long ago.

BBH: Ooh, what was that then?

ETT: Posing for the Anglers Monthly, something to do with trying to attract more women into fishing. She said it was ok, but she didn't like having to hold that big pike.

[Pause]

BBH: I've never liked fish. They're not to be trusted.

ETT: Our Malc don't like me to put fish in the fridge.

BBH: Where are you supposed to put it then?

ETT: No. I mean if I buy it I have to use it on the day I buy it. He says he doesn't like to be threatened by fish.

BBH: I know what he means.

[Pause]

ETT: Our Phil's mate Jack, his brother Luke is getting married in a couple of weeks. The grandkids are really looking forward to it.

BBH: How old are they now, Doreen?

ETT: Sally's seven and Poppy's four, can't believe it, time does fly. They aren't bridesmaids, just guests, got their outfits sorted. Got them here actually. [Lowers her voice] It's one of them same sex dos.

BBH: Ooh right.

ETT: Our Poppy said she didn't know two men could get married. Kids, eh.

BBH: Ooh, what did you say?

ETT: I said that you can marry anyone you like as long as you love 'em.

BBH: That was quick thinking.

ETT: Not quick enough. She then said she loved her dad, her sister and the hamster and wanted to marry 'em all.

BBH: Where are they getting wed?

ETT: At that Unilateral Church on Edward Road.

BBH: Are you going to watch?

ETT: Yes, I want to see who throws the bouquet. [Laughs]

[Pause]

BBH: What times your lunch break, Doreen? Are you 12 or 1?

ETT: I'm 12 today. I'm off to try to catch the Asda opening, just to see what all the fuss is about. They said they were giving away free samples.

BBH: Oh right, I might pop up on my break just to have a nosey.

[Request from the changing room]

ETT: [Puts on posh voice] Oh dear, madam, 14 no good, I know the sizes these days are perceiving. Yes, they do skimp on fabric. I'll look to see if we have a 16, madam. You sit tight.

The Protection Proposal

This is a clandestine meeting between a bee and a wasp. The bee is a British aristocratic type who talks with a very posh accent and looks down on wasps as inferior in every way. The wasp is an American con artist type character, uneducated but streetwise and crafty.

Wasp: I need to talk to you, man.

Bee: What an earth have I got to discuss with the likes of you?

W: You see that is exactly what I want to talk to you about. Your attitude and what we can do to improve Wasp/Bee relations.

B: What do you mean my attitude? You are the one with attitude, everybody knows that. You give insects that have the capability to sting a bad name. As for wasp/bee relations I think we are quite happy with the way things are thank you.

W: Whadya mean, man? I sting because I must - when I feel threatened, when those pesky humans get too close with their sprays and swatters. I don't have no choice, it's a survival thing, man. Survival of the fittest, fastest or the stingiest.

B: There is no such word as stingiest.

W: There is now, man, I just invented it. Ha ha. Anyway, man, what I want to discuss is a possible truce between us. I know you look down on us wasps as inferior to you, but I think it's time for an insect entente cordial if you know what I mean. We ain't that bad and I think if we joined forces we could ensure a safe and productive future. Well, productive to you anyway, we don't really do no producing.

B: And what could possibly be in this for bees?

W: Look brother, it makes perfect sense. You need protecting, you is a species in danger. It's on every wildlife programme, in those big Sunday papers with shiny supplements and the right on naturist are on the case planting things you like and not letting humans get rid of you when you build a nest. It's all out there, brother. It ain't no secret you is in endangerment.

B: I think you mean naturalist, naturists are the ones who like to go around naked. Also, we are endangered.

W: OK, ok, endangered. Anyway, I had a word with the brethren and we is offering our services. We figured if we protect you this will in turn protect us. 'Cause you are the ones that everyone loves. You hear the mommas telling their kids 'Don't' kill bees they make honey and are good for the environment, but wasps they are pests.' There is even laws to protect you bees. No laws for us, brother.

B: Will you stop calling me brother, I am not your brother!

W: Figure of speech, man, I guess we are both stinging creatures, we both fly, we are both kinda stripy and we both have families to support and struggle to survive. The difference is you are a victim of carelessness and stupidity, even neglect. I am a victim of vindictiveness and hate.

B: You do ask for it sometimes, you know. Your sting is pretty awful, I have seen the results and people don't know what you contribute. What do you contribute? What do you bring to the party?

W: What do you mean? We bring lots to the party. We bring a buzz. A swirl of colour. A frisson of danger. Even that pop star got his name from us

B: Sting, you mean Sting? I beg to differ, old chap. I think you will find he was called Sting after a sweatshirt of black and yellow stripes he was fond of which made him look like a bee.

W: It made him look like a wasp, mister clever clogs. Anyway back to my proposal. What do you think? Protection for your hives. Security for wasps. No strings, or stings. Ha ha, it's a win, win idea. What do you say? Come on are you in?

B: You forget, my dear boy, we have protocols to follow. You know I have to take it to the Queen and our security section for a decision. I can't simply say yes, let's go ahead. She is the one who will decide, and I have to say she is not a big wasp fan after the incident last year. We don't like being implicated in stings that are nothing to do with us. However, I will try to convince her that this would be a short term, mutually beneficial arrangement which could help with our growth and survival. I will return when I have spoken to her and let you know what she says.

W: Security, you got James Bond on board to advise then? OK, man, but this offer is only gonna be on the table for 48 hrs. I think you need us more than we need you. Our protection business is growing and if you dawdle, we may not have the wasp power to fulfil the offer anyway.

 Aside: Put that in your pipe and smoke it you stuck up buzzer.

B: Very well I will request an audience with the Queen as soon as possible and get back to you.

W [Aside]:The Queen will never countenance being involved with those pointy-tailed buzzers. They are common as muck and twice as dangerous. Not to be trusted and I shall advise her of such. We have survived this long without them, and I think we can manage a few millennia more.

My Sister

You always refused to conform, didn't you? When mother tried to curl your hair or dress you in frilly frocks, you pouted and sulked until you were allowed back into your dungarees or shorts (depending on the weather). As you got older you told Mam that you didn't want to be 'glammed up'. Of course, she took that to mean neglect, but worse than that, not good marriage material.

There was talk, of course. I didn't understand being nearly two years younger, but one day a friend of mine talked about a woman she knew being a 'shirt and tie job'. I was clueless and when she explained, I could not believe it, but gradually the idea of you like that became a fixture in my mind.

I don't think you were 'a shirt and tie job' I think you were a very precise, self-contained person who was very comfortable in their own skin. To you the problem did not lie with you but with those who judged you.

In those days of course anything that slipped outside of society's strict boundaries of normal was viewed with suspicion and intolerance. Your saving grace was that you were clever and subsequently successful. You secured a good job with the

Civil Service and with your precision and inner confidence you climbed the career ladder.

Mother tried to be proud but really she was bewildered and out of her depth. She didn't really know or understand women like you. I ticked the boxes for her: I married; gave her grandchildren, and visited regularly. I was happy and content for most of the time, although I often wondered what your life was like. Your freedom and your independence fascinated me and scared me at the same time.

You were happy, at least I think you were. It was hard to say sometimes. You've gone now, of course, and I realise that what you did was what so many of us wanted to do, but didn't dare. You were an unlikely trailblazer, but utterly true to yourself. Although I rarely saw you, I miss you. I miss saying I have an older sister and bragging about your differentness your success. You instinctively knew the right path for you and would not be swayed. You stuck to your guns when it would have been easier to give in and I admire and love you for that.

Sign of the Times

Sarah didn't give a damn what anybody else thought, she loved it. She glanced down at her arm as she wheeled Dorothea into the conservatory. The petal of the rose looked so real and the way the stem curled around her wrist and arm the cascading leaves scattered along the way, just wonderful.

She stopped the wheelchair near the window where the Autumn sunshine engulfed the room. Dorothea lifted her face up to the warmth and light. Sarah smiled and put her hand on Dorothea's shoulder. Sarah loved looking after Dorothea, despite being in her nineties she was such a lively, positive, person and was always interested in the world and the people who surrounded her.

'So, what have you been up to on your days off?' enquired Dorothea.

'Nothing much, just the usual stuff you know, cleaning, cooking, washing and all that jazz.' Sarah did the 'jazz hands' as she spoke, making Dorothea smile.

'Oh, I'm forgetting. I did get a new adornment on Thursday,' Sarah quipped.

'What do you mean another adornment?' asked Dorothea.

'Another tat,' said Sarah.

She turned her arm and showed Dorothea.

Dorothea tutted, but smiled at the same time in a way that, whilst showing some disapproval, also admired Sarah's 'go for it' attitude. Girls are different these days.

'Do you like it? I think its bloody lovely. The trouble is some people have this attitude towards tattoos. I saw a sign in the window of Ink Addiction. It said, "You don't like my tattoos? Well, I don't like your face." Does that mean we should cover that up too? Honestly, some people are so prejudiced and think we are all thugs.'

Dorothea giggled. 'How many have you got now?' she asked.

Sarah pretended to count, 'Five so far, but I don't think I have stopped yet.'

'Do you think you might regret getting them when you are older?'

'Hell no,' said Sarah, 'I think they will remind me of my youth, of the good times, my friends, important times in my life, all that sort of stuff.'

'Shall we smuggle you out and get you one, Dorothea? I can see you with a tasteful butterfly on your ankle or a dove, something sophisticated.'

Dorothea looked up at Sarah, 'You might be surprised to hear that I already have one.'

'No way,' Sarah's eyes widened, and she winked at Dorothea, 'Let's have a look then. Come on, you dark horse.'

Dorothea looked up at Sarah and suddenly became quiet.

Sarah was confused, 'Come on you wild thing, let's see.'

Dorothea looked up again and as she did, she slowly unrolled her left sleeve. There on her forearm was a number.

'Oh,' said Sarah, 'I'm not being rude, Dorothea, but it's not exactly art, is it? Not very symbolic like.'

Dorothea looked away. Where to start?

Marcus Nolan

They Usually Come to Me in the End

"Ooh, who trod on her foot?"
"Fancy - dentists, even in those days!"

No end of inanities here - they all forget my history and the violence around my slaying. Slicing my head off, if you please.

I never liked that Perseus, he really got ahead of himself, if you pardon my pun. All par for the course for Michelangelo Caravaggio – Micky loved a bit of roughhousing. Donning his cape late at night, he got up to no good in Rome, Malta, Naples and Sicily, swinging his sword and looking for trouble.

Of course, they were all vying for attention, these painters, artists and stone-cutters.

Nice of old Francesco though, to give my portrait to Ferdinand Medici, as if he needed reminding of my decapitation.

Those days everybody liked a beheading. What about that Assyrian General Holofernes, who didn't get where he was by being nice to the *hoi polloi*? Right up Putin's street.

It was butter-wouldn't-melt-in-my-mouth Judith, who neatly dispatched him by giving him some cleavage, right round the neck after a wild party. Be careful who you drink with, even if they are pretty, that's what I say.

Yes, rubbing out your enemies, how about a nice picture for the living room. You know, the results of another necktie party with an eccentric preacher from the desert. The violence continues into the New Testament, courtesy of that Trump-like Herod.

"You can have anything you want, honey, it's on me."

"Right, I want the head of that mad John the Baptist, who dissed us in public"

At least the Maltese have that one, in Valletta Cathedral of all places.

And then, "Let's get in with Jehovah and show young irreproachable Isaac the knife." Never mind that Daddio wasn't required to do the deed, it was the thought that counted. Micky put that down on canvas too!

See, you've got me started, but I suppose I'm entitled, being part of a long string of exterminations.

Of course there's David and Goliath and Micky did that one as well. But, here's the thing, it's all very well gawping at me here in the Uffizi - try going over the street to that Academia joint. First floor, I dare you. You'll not get far with that lot in a frenzy for snaps. A sea of arms outstretched seeking that perfect camera angle.'

Who needs fences? They make a photographic palisade as they jostle, their gaze fixated on the resident giant figure. Too busy with the click and ping of phones to ensure their zany angles of the smooth, shadowy face and then missing the cleverly concealed weapon.

What's that thing on his shoulder? *No, it's* **not** a scarf - he killed Goliath because of it! Talk about stoned!

Anyhow that one wasn't Micky, it was another Michelangelo, di Lodovico Buonarroti Simoni if you must know. He captured David for posterity, all 14 foot of him.

Take it or leave it, but I could never stand white marble – it's stone all the way for me.

Sunday in Devon

To Churston Ferrers church at 9.30 am

Gentle, country Anglicanism at its friendliest, the six bells of St Mary the Virgin sounding a clear welcome outside. Inside there are plenty of white heads, with an expectant cheerfulness suffusing the well-filled box pews. Angela from Essex, recently retired from the choir, bravely admitting to failing vocal chords, expressed her regret at not relocating earlier to Devon and its much easier quality of life. She couldn't, however, extend her enthusiasm to the vertiginous slopes of Brixham, preferring the more horizontal Paignton.

This 14th century church, in perpendicular style, was well lit by plain and stained glass, a mixture of the usual hues, the most recent donated by the author Agatha Christie. Her altar window by James Patterson of Bideford, was a delightful blend of mauve and light greens depicting Jesus as the Good Shepherd.

News from the parish pump was declaimed by a confident suntanned layman. Then a sizeable choir disgorged itself up the tiny aisle and completely filled the choir stalls. They were followed by a greying priest more than successfully occupying his chasuble. His well dissembled Liverpool origins occasionally emerged during the sermon, when his extempore discourse hit a note of even greater enthusiasm. Befitting the name of the church, he tackled the set gospel of the day, intriguingly exploring the unlikely plight of the perplexed Mary. She was to later confound received theological wisdom, but meanwhile found solace with an elderly relative, also catapulted into a mysterious pregnancy.

Following the post-service social interlude, I declined parish coffee and took mine next door instead in the ancient hostelry which belonged to the Yarde family from 15th to 18th Century. It exuded a centuries old patina of hospitality but also that inexplicable expectancy that some famous character might emerge from behind a heavy brocade   curtain and either challenge you to a duel or offer you a drink.

I settled for reading the paper on the terrace before setting out for the ferry to Dartmouth.

There was that eerie feeling that something, but not you, rather the scenery, is moving.   It made me realise that the modern mechanism for grabbing two sunken cables and hauling many tons of craft and vehicles had already furtively propelled us more than a third of the way across the Dart.

For the nonchalant natives this happens over 150 times daily but for me, the brief ride ending, as the road literally rose up to meet us was a welcome portent - an announcement that, by this modest river crossing, the holiday had truly begun.

Seeing a car park on the right, I trusted my instincts and found the modern marina not a horrid plastic imposition but a sophisticated haven for the seeker of outstanding service and exceptional food – who needs boats?

To Dartmouth Marina for lunch al fresco

Seated at an outside table I savoured my second coffee of the morning from an aromatic cafetiére of an exceptionally robust blend. Gazing across the harbour was an experience close to the numinous, watching the countless boats and ferries with their relentless traffic. Steam trains trailed their vapour parallel to the water, echoing hoots heralding their arrivals.

Lunch was called for, and as I lingered over the options, Kostas hovered and I was not disappointed by difficult choices from a replete menu. Zoltan was the bringer of ham and chicken terrine with homemade apple and ginger chutney, sweet beetroot juice, apricot and walnut bread and the initial part of a mandatory luncheon rosé. This I dallied over.

As the ending came to the delectable appetiser, all was not lost, Zoltan made the correct pincer movement with another plate. This time fondant potato of the most inviting, burnished kind bid me welcome, and nestling aside its grandeur, pan-fried bream and fresh vegetables with a nearly concealed verdant cream sauce, set to seduce my taste buds further.

Should a man wish for another wave of lusciousness? I had mercifully already committed to the wonderful shiny chocolate ganache, accompanied by home-made milk ice cream, roofed with salted caramel sauce. How strange that this should take such a time to consume....

I exchanged pleasantries with a well-coutured lady on the next table. She was waiting for her daughter having undeclared spa treatment. Meanwhile, Henry Greenwood, a descendant of Bess of Hardwick, took her place and waxed lyrical. His focus was the Marina kitchen and then the position and joy that was Dartmouth (where he lived most of the time when not staying in Park Lane or Derbyshire). Clearly a Gentleman of Leisure, he asked if I had plans to dine at the Winking Prawn in Salcombe and, on a literary note, whether I had read much about Marcel Proust on food.

The answer was no but as he wandered off in search of his next diversion, I knew I must delve into Proust's *In Search of Lost Time.* For him, eating is a process that transforms the substance and appearance of food into something beyond mere consumption - "a delight for the imagination and for the eye".

"the spiced beef jellies are transparent blocks of quartz;
the asparagus, with their celestial hues, exquisite creatures which assumed vegetable form; the potatoes, Japanese ivory buttons; the cherries in the boat-shaped tartlets are

beads of corals changed into something precious by the azure sky"

To Dartmouth Citadel for an afternoon walk

Meandering around Dartmouth I took in the fort at Bayard's Cove artillery, constructed in 1634, where eleven gun ports, in solid walls, overlooked the most strategic part of the mouth of the Dart. Now, they concealed cooing sweethearts murmuring messages to each other.

Here was where the ill-fated Speedwell expedition to the Americas left British shores around 17 years earlier. Three years later in 1620, the guiding hand of Elder William Brewster, possibly one of my forebears on my mother's Winward side, led a historically famous and more successful departure on The Mayflower.

Winding my way back to the car via a traditional park with banks of flowers and lawn-sprawled teenagers and children, I watched small and large boats navigate the river, sails and engines alternately deferring and asserting rights over the constant cursor of the ferry. In the shallows young seagulls played, their parents with half an eye on unwary ice cream eaters on the banks above.

This led me to my first haiku, or an approximation of it, of the holiday:

Grey gull chick
On round buoy
Doomed to dive

To Dartington for cultural treats

I aimed the car up country, through Totnes.

I had booked, at late notice, a concert of Flute, Bassoon and Piano. This was to be in the inspiring great vaulted hall of the extraordinary estate of Dartington. According to Pevsner, it is one of the most spectacular surviving domestic buildings of late Medieval England. It currently is home to the Dartington Arts School with Masters programmes, including Arts and Place, Arts and Ecology and Poetics of Imagination.

Unwittingly, I had appeared at the height of the Dartington Annual Summer School and was transported, in this afternoon concert, into soothing melodies by Debussy, Dutilleux and Louise Farrenc. Farrenc was the first female director of the Paris Conservatoire and for the initial ten years of her 30 year Victorian tenure, fought an eventually successful battle for equal pay .... *courage mon brave*. But there would have been no contest on an equal stage as she composed over 30 piano pieces, and also numerous chamber, choral and orchestral works into the bargain.

After that, what can one do?

In my case, I sauntered around the manicured gardens, and amongst other things, observed a perfectly coiffured, suntanned woman of maturity. She was standing on a stone bench looking into a 15 foot-high hedge dressed in what looked like a white damask nightgown. With a cut-glass accent, she was assisting her obsessive nine year-old grandson who had been hunting interminably for various fauna in the bushes:

Young explorer squeaks: "I'm absolutely positive it is still here, Granny."

Granny sighs: "Well I think perhaps we should leave it for the moment, Tristan darling, and perhaps come back later."

Following a visionary moment with the fountain of caressing swans with a barely energised jet of water, I sensed my sensual and beauty-filled summer's day was nearly complete. But, it was not to be as two further haiku style poems surfaced, one inspired by wildlife, on a planted lead cistern:

Snacking rabbit
Covertly cowering
Under bronze Acer

the other by an immaculately trimmed and raked Zen garden:

The flat bush
Like a tall pill
Nestles by stones

We left the estate with the tower of St Mary's on the left. After Totnes, with the supposedly haunted Berry Pomeroy Castle up in the distance, the car seemed to float back to the cliff tops of Brixham.

As the evening sun smiled, and under the apple trees, tapas and vino verde completed the enchantment of a perfect summer interlude.

"The real voyage of discovery consists, not in seeking new landscapes, but in having new eyes."

Marcel Proust

A Garden Villanelle
Seasonal dreaming of nature's ratio

The gardener dreams of horticultural structure
Dark winter's light showing growth only lean
It has to be right for the border.

So seedsman's delight and conscious conjecture
With spring's new season displaying it's green
At the end of the choosing there has to be order.

Now landscaping depiction of earth's recent fracture
The unfurling of leaves revealing verdigris sheen
It has to be right for the border.

Legs that dig and unleash loam's infrastructure
Bring forth the colours of summer's lush dene
At the end of the choosing there has to be order.

Insistently and often the pruner's restructure
To develop with vigour the solstice time's scene
It has to be right for the border.

Then autumn bright nights with flowering stricture
Moon shines it's prospect crisp, white and keen
At the end of the choosing there has to be order.
It has to be right for the border.

Mike O'Sullivan

In the Beginning Man Created God

I can't remember how long I had spent in the field hospital. Time had slowed down. Was it weeks or months? It is hard to tell. All of us were waiting for something to happen. As for me, I just sat and watched. Watching was the only thing I could do there. Young boys came and went. The ones who left went out in coffins. I knew that the Commander had been wounded. It surprised me. I thought he was immortal. I remember how all of us put on a brave face whereas he seemed to be revelling in it. He liked killing the enemy. He said that it made him feel like God.

The power of life and death.

I had taken a walk outside for a cigarette. There wasn't much else to do. There was a group of lads sitting outside the tent.

I could tell from the look on their faces that they had been through what I had been through. I sit down, I light a cigarette and watch them. Yes, they are like me. They have nothing to do apart from remember. Memory lane, memory pain.

One of them is lying down on the grass. They have brought him out here. He looks badly wounded. He probably doesn't have long to go. Then I see the Commander approach him. I hadn't seen him since he brought me here. I watch him crouch down next to the boy. He is whispering something to him. His voice is quiet, but I can just hear his words. He is telling him that very soon the suffering will be over.

Soon he will be in Heaven. I can't understand why he is doing this. It doesn't make sense. He hates the Church. I remember him saying he is an atheist.

"In the beginning Man created God."

I watch him finish and walk away. I follow him. He stops and turns around. I ask him why he hasn't been to see me. He tells me that he just wanted to get better, so that he could go back to the front line. I'm curious. I want to know why he was talking about God when he doesn't believe in his existence.

In times like this there is no common sense. Once you understand this then you understand what the reality of war is. There is only one truth, and it doesn't matter if you are an atheist or a believer. Everyone fears death. I don't know how anyone can deal with the fact that their life will soon come to an end. That boy is scared because he is dying. Maybe it is better to die believing in a lie. Why is all of this happening? I must give him an answer. I know that God is an illusion, but we all need illusions. You must give people hope even when you know how brittle it can be. I know that I am saying these things to you because I want to hear it myself.

I think about the lives that I have ended. The first time I killed someone was at the start of this war. I shot a boy. For a time afterwards, I used to see his face in my dreams. It is really something you know. Killing a human being. That life is all he has. It's all he'll ever have. I don't have the dreams now.

I hate what I have become. If you asked me what that boy looked like I could not tell you. His face just fades into all the other faces. I talk to myself all the time. I tell myself not to think about the consequences of my actions. We all fought for a cause, didn't we? I thought that the cause would absolve me of the sin of killing someone.

I know that it's a lie because the other side has the same thoughts. If God exists, he is playing a game with us that we don't understand. Sometimes I wonder whether there is something deeply rooted in me. Maybe I was always like this. There is a bad seed in me. If God does exist, then I will try to make my case. I will give my reasons. I doubt somehow that he will listen. There is one thing I know for certain though.

If he does exist, then I am not going to Heaven.

Sarah Payler

By Night We Danced

Under a low hung city moon,
trees decorated firefly bright,
I watched you dance.
Sinuous, strong, mesmerising,
how I envied your willowy partners.

Dance with me you said taking my hand,
my protest silenced with a look.
Spellbound I followed your moves,
step, step, glide, step, step, turn.
The beginning of our own unique rhythm.

All that long hot summer,
busy lives punctuated by sultry nights,
you taught me to quickstep and waltz.
Rustic versions of ballroom polish,
danced to guitar, accordion and drum.

Life compressed in those snatched hours,
between dusk and dawn.
Closed embraces hip to hip,
we mastered the rhumba and the tango.
As we choreographed a time of our own.

Summer slipped into cool autumn.
Our last dance a perfected foxtrot,
starlit amongst falling leaves.
Carelessly we whirled and slowed,
to the rise and fall of another life.

No more falling asleep exhausted,
to the lullaby of a dawn chorus.
As our flawless steps faltered,
amid a lament of entwined limbs.
To embrace the dance of a different day.

Have a Nice Day

A throaty purr of an orange and blue bus, a cheery, black-bearded driver.

A woman, an early bird, a buttoned up cardi, a tartan shopper.

A uniform creased Care Worker going home, a whiff of tobacco and soap.

A would-be poet anticipates a weekly shopping trip and a treat.

A gaggle of girls, plaid skirts, heads down, diligently studying phones.

A lone schoolboy, a pair of grubby socks, big headphones, mouths silent words.

A stop at a hospital, a stubbly man, a sad face, a crutch, a carrier bag.

A bus station in all its morning glory, awash with cheap floral disinfectant.

A calm waterway. A gentle breeze. A pervasive aroma of wet earth and weed.

A prehistoric heron perches on a river pole; a fish patiently waits to be caught.

A tall woman in horn-rimmed glasses flies along a towpath on a green bike.

A helmet of grey hair, streaked kingfisher blue, a drawing tube over one shoulder.

A walk in the park, a wood pigeon sits in a Silver Birch and coos to a mate.

A blue bench with white daisies, an elderly couple its first guests of the day.

A metallic clank of a kiosk shutter, a smell of coffee, bacon and freshly cut grass.

A bandy-legged man on a short walk, a polite dog, no balls thrown today.

A short-necked man in an office, huffs and puffs and dispenses a train ticket.

A delayed 'O', nine, 'O', six train, now due to depart at 'O', nine, 'O', nine.

A slow train hisses to a stop, a collective sigh of commuting passengers.

A disheartened man on a mobility scooter tries to board a busy carriage.

A buzzard, a field, a house, an impatient red car, a station, a blur of speed.

A child in a straw hat, with cat ears and whiskers, a pair of well-behaved grandparents.

A loud couple roll cigarettes with practiced precision, on their way to a Family Court.

A rhythmic ebb and flow of conversation, a train ambles on to its next destination.

A melee of passengers disgorges and embarks, a bulky case crashes into a shin.

A nose assailed, a bouquet of shower gel, sweat, hot metal and city dust.

A crowded concourse, an overpriced fast-food outlet – not a time to dawdle.

A pigeon walks into a hire-car booth! *(there's a joke in there – somewhere)*.

A day tripper worries over a direction to take, a fare to choose.

A ticket inspector with a frown, trundles up a platform, he's here to help!

A skinny teen pours abuse into a phone. A shimmer of anger and heat.

A man runs across a track, a travel-pass pings. A tram glides to a halt.

An unforgiving strapless top, a tight skirt, an England shirt, a surplus of baggy shorts.

A fake tan, a pair of bingo wings, a parade of lily-white legs, a crazed network of blue veins.

A Big Issue seller, a wide-eyed street beggar, a blue cocooned rough sleeper.

A silent e-scooter weaves wildly, a curse, yet another cool-bag brunch.

A welcome relief of artificial coolness, a comforting 'go to' high-street brand.

A vista of summer-ready linen, a choice of hot orange, olive green, crisp white.

A smiley shop worker, a new top in an eco-friendly bag - 'an e-receipt OK love?'

Joyce has worked for M&S for over twenty years, she's retiring – Have a Nice Day!

The Puppet

They said she must attend and if today were to be a day of reckoning, she believed she was ready. Truthfully her curiosity had got the better of her and the guilt of enjoying the performance about to unfold was minor in comparison to her many sins. Her cover story, if asked, would be to introduce herself as Lucy's Great Aunt Isabella, on her father's side. Concealed by excellent make-up and well-placed padding she was unrecognisable, although the black veil and silver-topped cane were maybe an affectation too far? As backup, her black suited minder was armed, she wasn't sure how comforting this was.

From the back of the Chapel her view was perfect and unlike her alto ego, her hearing sharply attuned and wary to mishap but, so far, everything had gone according to plan, indeed she'd say almost reassuringly so. The setting was not one of her choosing, utilitarian, with high windows, insipid furnishings and a hint of sterility. Maybe in her next life she would re-embrace the Catholicism of her youth, its ceremonies imbibed with ritual and mysticism and churches redolent with the aroma of fragrant incense and beeswax.

Her maternal cousins had turned up to pay their respects, in the hope of a pay-out, no doubt. She watched Cousin Roger and his wife Marisa, two parsimonious, black-garbed crows, chittering away at the family solicitor. They were in for a bitter disappointment as her supposed wealth had been grossly exaggerated and never intended for them.

Other than the cousins and interspersed with more anonymous, black-suited personnel, were her former acquaintances and associates. The men in rarely worn black ties, white shirts and dark suits; the high heeled women in an array of funeral chic. Never a group to knowingly pass up a chance to be seen or to partake in salacious gossip over a free Prosecco or two. Gossip was already rife regarding the likelihood of 'the husband' benefitting from her untimely demise, certainly given his current whereabouts.

Her best friend, Alice Morgan and her neighbour, Mrs. Hudson were also here, probably the only genuine mourners. Alice, bless her, in her customary pink, a flamingo in a sea of corvids and bosomy Mrs. Hudson, pearls at her neck, squeezed into her best tweed. Guilt rose in her chest like acid and a tear rolled down her powdered cheek, caught up in all the chaos and drama she had forgotten those she cared for most. It had been one of the hardest things, in this whole business, not to say goodbye. Both would receive a modest financial gift, but that was not enough, this was forever.

With a change of tempo in the music piped through discreet speakers, the coffin arrived, covered in a spray of overripe lilies. The chatter ceased, and everyone stood. She tried not to think of the contents confined to the plain casket, information withheld from her. Aware of a palpable shockwave rippling through the room she looked up. Following the coffin was Charlie, handcuffed between two warders. Never a large man, his once immaculate suit hung from his shoulders, but he had lost none of his innate swagger. Perhaps because she was staring, he stopped and turned, looking directly at her. Was this the feared reckoning? He knew, she was sure of it.

Her ears buzzed, the sweet stench of lilies hit the back of her throat and a wave of nausea engulfed her; why was he here? They had said he would not, under any circumstances, be given permission to attend. She had been very clear NO lilies, NO Charlie.

Afterwards she remembered little of the celebrant's platitudes or Alice's heartfelt poem. Only Charlie's eulogy, full of mawkish sentiments, insincere regrets and downright lies, stuck in her head. A firm hand on her arm had prevented her from leaping up to protest and as the casket slid behind the curtain her minder helped her to her feet and they slipped out of the chapel.

Whilst relieved at fulfilling her side of the bargain, she was frustratingly left with unanswered questions. What was the purpose behind her being here? Why had Charlie come to a funeral to grieve for a woman he had never loved and who had betrayed him? Yes, he was guilty, but not of the crime he was serving time for, that was her misdeed alone.

Outside the Black Alfa Romeo was waiting to take her to St. Pancras and the next Eurostar. In it someone who might respond to her questions, but as expected, she was not to be enlightened. Her contact known to her only as Signor Caruso, furnished her with a new passport, health and travel documents and money, but no answers. Instead, a hitch of the shoulder and his stock response, "Signora, I'm just the messenger, not the 'maestro delle marionette'."

As the car pulled away, Charlie was leaving the chapel, struggling against his captors. Later she would wonder if she had imagined the sound of a gunshot or seeing him crumple to the ground, a bloom of red seeping across his white shirt. She would never be sure, and no one would ever tell her the truth of it.

In the weeks to come, as she waited in a smart apartment in a Naples, she would realise she had been both naïve and foolish to think it was all over. Caruso had handed her a burner phone saying, "We have another job for you Lucia, someone will be in touch." And she would bitterly recall the sadness of her Mama's tears and her Papa's shrugged responses; "What can I do, Cara? Once in debt to The Mob, always in debt to The Mob."

Mark Pringle

Alter Ego

He closed the laptop and looked out into the garden. Not much to do there now, too cold, too dead. Autumn was getting into its stride; decay was winning the seasonal battle. There was that misty, damp, rotting leaves atmosphere in the air; the sun a watery eye and low.

Mary would be home from work at five. Then they would join the crowds doing the Friday weekly shop, playing dodgems with the trolley, examining purchases minutely, and waiting ages at the checkout. Joining the rush hour traffic, thirty minutes to do one and a half miles. He could have ordered everything online, then they would stay in, but that was not what they did. 'I'm not having their nearly out of date stuff foisted on me and they always substitute things they want to get shut of,' she would state. Then there will be the immovable stress fest of unpacking and getting the dinner on at the same time. Why wouldn't it be better to stay in, light the fire, have a drink and get the supper at leisure? Well…yes...

Just now he had been replying to an e-mail. He didn't usually send e-mails to Florida. He didn't usually discover more relations in North America, but that is where his on-line genealogical research had led him. He had been having another discussion with Jim, a recently discovered second cousin. Jim was chatty, open, relaxed, enjoying his life, good humoured, called him friend and cousin. He knew more about the family history than anyone in the UK, shared everything, was on top of the detail, not bogged down by it.

When he sent Jim a very neutral photo of Mary and himself standing a foot apart from each other in the garden, both wearing inscrutable faces, Jim wrote back saying he liked the photo, 'you both look like real British!' But then Jim shares genes with me; we are partly identical, he pondered. From now on his train of thought developed in a direction that didn't include the Friday shop. A distant relation with a bit of me in him might be living in the Florida Keys, say as a writer: free, independent, flying down to stay for months at a time in his second home by the Gulf of Mexico. It could be an alternative me, say I emigrated ages ago. What would such a person, me, be called, maybe, Scott, well why not? Yes, what would a new day, a new dawn, look like?

Crimson, gold, purple, the vibrant sky show in the East brings in a new day, the colours stream in though the open shutters. I arrived back in Key South late last night, a week before Christine. This is my first morning back for a while. Rise early, shower; shorts, tee shirt, sandals. Go downstairs put coffee on, juice, fruit. I take the coffee to my desk by a window, set it down to brew. Have a walk round the garden, partially shaded by palms, fragrance from the blooms already wafting past on the warm birdsong filled breeze, the vibrant colours of Bougainvillea and Desert Rose changing against the brightening blue sky. Looking back at the house: historic, two storeys, whitewashed, with pale yellow shutters and black wrought iron balcony and veranda front and back. This is going to be a good day; the difficult transition chapter should be finished by midday. The critics think Scott is having problems with his latest. Not now, not with this change of scene, I can feel the words pulling at me to be written, the old excitement.

The morning drifts by quickly as the writing is going well. The southern light and fresh warm sea breeze spur me on. E-mail from Lev next door, he will be in The Captain's Bar at twelve. More coffee and a final thousand words, it's done! Around twelve I leave the house; shades and hat needed now the sun is high. Walk along the street past the villas and gardens, say hi to a couple of neighbours out front. 'Hi Scot,' they reply. Turn into Main, past the white clapboard St

Joseph's Church, the pink, sage green and blue painted stores and dive shops, all busy with business and customers then into The Captain's Bar on the next corner. Inside it is spacious, cool, with traditional ceiling fans and cane furniture leading up to a carved bar with a shrine to crystal behind it. "Hi Scott". It's Lev at the bar, we catch up on the last couple of months, I get the usual digs for not being here for most of the hurricane season. Meanwhile, Alexi the maestro, is mixing our drinks, a performance we both respectfully keep one eye on. When he's finished, he presents them to us. The Key Lime Martinis glow lime in frosted glasses on the bar, beautiful fragrance rising elegantly from them. After savouring the Martinis, it's a Cuban sandwich and an equally frosted beer. We take the beers out back and sit on benches looking over the turquoise and jade sea to the outlying Keys. Lev regales me with stories from his tough New York upbringing, he is a successful writer too. 'Take our past and turn it into your future, it owes you,' he says.

After leaving Lev, I return home and take it easy on the back veranda, scribble a few ideas down and doze off mid-afternoon. Later, I leave the house and turn away from Main to where my street gives out to beach. White sand, palms, quiet now. I walk slowly into the mild water, so clear to look down into it is almost invisible, but for the gentle ripples and the splash of the waves, the re-assuring music of calm water. Swimming you become detached, released and at the same time buoyed, supported and cradled. The sun waves around like it is on a stick above you. Below multi-striped colourful fish float and dart around coral of crusty shape and form in bronze, red, purple and orange. A cormorant standing on a nearby rock flaps its wings. I float for what seems like ages but is probably only a few minutes soaking up the feeling of the moment, timeless warm now.

Back home another shower, change. Downstairs, fix a salad and cold drink, catch up on e-mails. Read for a while on the front balcony, watch people, wave at some, show them

I'm back, soak up the feeling of community, sense the pulse of the town as it moves through late afternoon, end of the working week. Tonight a group of us are going to one of the uninhabited keys close by for a barbecue.

Early evening, I walk through town. The atmosphere has changed now, the sun is lower, people are gathering for the evening, and are sitting outside, some relaxed, some, the young immortal girls and boys, anticipating a party. I arrive at the jetty where people are boarding the boat which will take us to the Key. We are a of collection of friends, acquaintances and a smattering of relatives, mostly active in the Arts, so it is a busman's holiday, but on a night like this, nobody is complaining. Colourful lanterns are strung around the boat, people walk around the deck to see what they look like illuminated in different shades, the ice is broken. Any left is in the drinks.

Soon we set off motoring serenely across the water, accompanied by a couple of dolphins, curious, curving in and out of the water, smiling, they too being illuminated by the different shades.

Landing on the Key we gather round the beach bar and then disperse onto the sand. Conversation and drink flow, the barbecue sizzles into life and is soon sending appetising incense among us. A mix of salsa and reggae music is added to the evening. As the light fades on the day the sunset streams with crimson, gold and purple, building to a crescendo and fading gently down into the sea. Just after dark a full moon rises out of the sea. Some now dance and sing, others move into the palms for privacy. Talk and bursts of laughter echo across the water. Soon, someone is swimming, when a shout goes up, there is luminescence in the water when a cloud appears in front of the moon. We paddle and swim and catch sight of a magician's electric blue fizzing almost to white, then the cloud passes and the moon returns. We go back to the party; some stay by the water.

After a few drinks, the perception of time floats, drifts on its own way unconcerned by the demands of the day. For a few moments we feel we could sail off with this island into infinity.

Time though arrives to board the boat and return to our jetty. A happy, but tired bunch sailing back under the lanterns. On the jetty good nights are said, a few go for night caps, one or two diehards fancy clubbing. I walk through the town, things have settled down now, there is relaxed and satiate feeling; it's the end of a good day and there are going to be more.

As I pass The Captain's Bar, Lev appears at the door and invites me in. 'Tomorrow maybe, not tonight I'm done,' I say. No, I'm heading home, anymore and I would end up like the now mortal girls and boys and ruin tomorrow. Who would want to do that in a place like this? I want to be up early, swim, then crack on with the next chapter; today has given me some good ideas. Anyway, the memory of those sparkling Key Lime Martini's on the bar will keep me going yet, till a new day, a new dawn.

"ERNEST! I'm back, you ready, make haste, or there'll be no bread left again", Mary shouts from the hallway. She goes into the kitchen after looking in the lounge, arranges some shopping bags.

"You should have gone to the toilet before I got back."

'ERNEST!'

"Where are you, you'll be the death of me."

Still no answer. She looks out into the garden, then goes to the foot of the stairs.

"ERNEST SCOTT WILLIAMS, ANSWER ME!"

No answer. She rushes back into the kitchen, sees Ernest's capsule bottles still by the kettle.

"Oh my God Ernie, you've gone out and left them again… where can you be?"

Words

Why do words
Trickle spill flow
Into a definite flood?

Scented image moon flower
Germinate seed grow
Balletic symphonic botany.

Sign refine define
Word by word by word
Forever a fugitive pursuit
Round and round
The walls of Jericho.

Cindy Rossiter

A Picture Paints

Green for calm
Brown for earth
Khaki for combat
Clothes for action
Face full of humour
Body full of power
His posture speaks of strength
His entire being of resolve
His back may be against the wall
But this man is not for moving

Beloved

In a peaceful pine forest in Tysum
Wooden crosses jostle for position

Here amongst the many lies Ludmilla
Beloved by Gregori

Her grave marked
by her number and a small purple wreath

Those whose task is to exhume
discover and document

Weep for their countrymen
Gregori weeps with them

Once Upon a Time…

Once upon a time
long long ago
you appeared
I held you close
looking forward to living
happily ever after
for I believed in fairy tales

Several years passed
disaster struck our world
over and over and over again
until suddenly one day
you were gone
And I was thrown into exile
in a land far far away

A lifetime later
I made my way back
still holding you close
These days though
my feet are leaden
I do not fly amongst the stars
and I no longer believe in fairy tales

The Smell of Hope

Vapour like
From deep inside
It rises
Growing
Building
Bursting free

An odour
All at once
Unusual and peculiar
Recognisable and familiar
Banished for some while
But here now

The smell of hope

What Makes Me Happy?

Family and the familiar
Far flung and the foreign
Art and the ambiguous
Champagne and celebrations
Roses and time to smell them
Being brain busy
Egos and the eccentric
Giving hope,
Having hope
A life in colour
Ability to laugh
And those who laugh with me
Irony
Poetry
Symmetry and the Abstract
Good food
Good wine
A good book
A good ending

The Contributors

Simon Allen His literary career began with self-published teenage poems noted for their excruciating angst and leaden wit. One was later published, sadly unattributed, in the literary journal at Hull University, where Simon once shared a lift with Philip Larkin. After a career writing court reports, which were rarely read, Simon can now be found in his local launderette, where he has embraced the post of *Poet in Residence*.

Mike Carter is a retired History teacher. He began writing with a WEA Creative Writing class in Beeston and has since enjoyed writing short stories, poetry and non-fiction. During the Covid Lockdown, he put together a collection of writing entitled *Pieces of Eight* with seven other members of the class. He has been a member of *Pen and Paper* since 2019. His other interests include art and family history.

Barry Cope trained as a polymer chemist and was employed in industry, both private and nationalised, before returning to academia. Post retirement, his literary interests are travel literature and memoir.

Roberta Dewa writes poetry, fiction and memoir, and is a published author in all three genres, with four published novels, a memoir, a short story in Salt's *Best of British 2021*, and poems in *Staple*, *Fin*, *The Coffee House,* and (forthcoming) *Acumen* and *Obsessed with Pipework*.

Elizabeth Dunford Her poems have been published in *Cannon's Mouth, Snakeskin, Silver Birch* and *Green Ink.* Her articles have been published in *Lapidus Journal* and in NAWE's *Writing in Education*. She is interested in the relationship between writing and well-being, and holds an MSc in Creative Writing for Therapeutic Purposes. She was born in India, grew up in Northern Ireland, and has lived in Nottingham for over thirty years.

Sue Gale enjoys writing memoir but, more recently, has written short stories which blend memoir with fiction. She is interested in the impact of childhood trauma on behaviour in later life and many of the plots in her stories reflect this theme. Her first book of short stories *Finally the Women Sing* was published in March.

Janet Gibson Her main interest in writing is memoir, short stories and dabbling with poetry. The Bromley House Library *Pen and Paper* group was a life saver during Covid times when they met on Zoom. The Group, who she has shared events and workshops with, have so enriched her life with warmth, humour and humanity.

Barry Harper is a retired police officer. He began writing in 2013 with the *Tin Hat Writers,* and subsequently *The Writer Highway* and *Pen & Paper.* He enjoys writing poetry, memoir and prose. He has been published in the Guardian newspaper and in several anthologies. His other interests include charity work, exercise, music and extreme adventures.

Julia Hodson just can't help writing dark comic fiction. Whatever structure the writing takes, poetry, monologue or short story she always deploys a generous dose of humour. Julia loves to edit and help others with their writing, but she really ought to get her own novel finished first.

Lindah Kiddey is a retired writer-editor-publicist for business, industry, education and the creative sectors. She admires short stories where brevity is king. Lindah's own efforts have been highly commended in national competitions, her poetry being published in a *Writer's Highway* collection and nationally online. She continues to write and read out her true-life tales to audiences at *tenx9* storytelling events.

Chris Niven has always enjoyed writing. She loves exploring different genres and techniques, and has been fortunate enough to have several pieces published. Working with other writers is always enriching and lively. The *Pen and Paper* group is certainly that! She looks forward to many more sessions of collaboration.

Marcus Nolan has experimented with a number of new genres, including the structure of the Villanelle and other poetry styles, including using different voices in his compositions. He greatly values writing in the moment, alongside stimulating literary colleagues and appreciates the shared conversational interludes at the Contemporary Café. Viva Bromley House Library!

Mike O'Sullivan is currently working as a cognitive behavioural psychotherapist. He has written two non-fiction works on psychotherapy, which have been published. After many years, he now recognises that there is more truth in fiction rather than non- fiction.

Sarah Payler As a child, Sarah loved to write stories, and was often teased about daydreaming. Retirement has encouraged her to re-visit her writing in both prose and poetry. She loves to people watch and to take a snapshot or an idea to see where her imagination leads her.

Mark Pringle His interest in reading returned after joining Bromley House Library in 2020. Amateur writing was the next step, and he joined the writing group. He thinks that things might have got a bit out of hand, having enrolled on an English Literature Certificate course with Oxford University.

Cindy Rossiter enjoyed poetry at school and has returned to it in recent years, seeing it both as creativity and therapy combined. She loves the challenge of expressing herself in as few words as possible. She has been lucky to have her poems inscribed on some local sculptures and to be published in a few places.

Pen and Paper Writers

Mike O'Sullivan

Sue Gale

Barry Cope

Marcus Nolan

Cindy Rossiter

Lindah Kiddey

Elizabeth Dunford

Robbie Dewa

Mike Carter

Julia Hodson

Simon Allen

Barry Harper

Chris Niven

Mark Pringle

Janet Gibson